Ruth Morgenegg
Appropriate care – a basic right for all rabbits

Ruth Morgenegg

Appropriate care – a basic right for all rabbits

Translated by
Trudy Hood and Sandra Collins

tbv

© tb-Verlag
Fax: +41 (0) 44 761 92 09
E-Mail: tb-verlag@bluewin.ch

1st edition 2009

Proofreading: Joan Kägi
Scan/Lithos: Walter Furrer, CH-8910 Affoltern am Albis
Print: printwork art gmbH

Printed in Germany

ISBN 978-3-9522661-2-0

Contents

Introduction by Andreas Steiger - Professor of
Animal Husbandry and Animal Welfare   7

How my passion for rabbits began   9
Dwarf rabbits are rabbits too   13

1. A short journey into the world of wild rabbits   15
2. Species-appropriate care should be more than just a statement   19
3. The basic needs of rabbits   23
4. Living outdoors – close to nature   33
5. The rabbit run – planning and building suggestions   45
6. Creating and maintaining an outside run   61

7. Living indoors – when reality demands compromise   77
8. Acquiring your new rabbits   93
9. The unique social behaviour   109

10. Reproduction and birth control   127
11. Nutrition and digestion   139
12. Health is no coincidence   153

13. Keeping rabbits and guinea pigs together   171

The rabbit and the area of controversy
between meat production animals and pets   177
If in doubt, ask!   179
A look behind the scenes of the Rabbit and
Rodent Refuge   189

Appendix   194
Index   195
The author and her work, by Marianne Wengerek   199

What we do to an animal today, we do to a living creature which has feelings, a creature whose spiritual life knows pain and pleasure like us, which can suffer more than we will ever know. We are therefore facing a new situation, as we now have more knowledge than ever before and therefore much greater responsibility.

Julie Schlosser

Introduction

According to a survey in Switzerland in 1994, 69% of people keeping pets were aware that rabbits need the company of other animals, but only 42% kept their own rabbits in groups. Similar results regarding guinea pigs and birds showed a lack of knowledge relating to the biological needs of various species, as well as a lack of care for pets.

Rabbits, especially dwarf rabbits, are favourite pets, but many are kept in inappropriate conditions all their life, due to a lack of knowledge regarding their real needs. Unfortunately, the knowledge of rabbits' real needs is still very restricted and, as the author says, "Education is essential".

Ruth Morgenegg, with her vast experience, passionately presents the basic needs of rabbits, with clear illustrations and writing. The correct keeping of rabbits, inside or outside, involves social contact with members of the same species, exercise, gnawing, digging, hiding places, a good overview within the run, variety and resting time. This book has many practical hints, questions from pet owners and photographs to assist the reader.

The Swiss Animal Welfare legislation regulates the keeping of dwarf rabbits, but this only consists of minimum requirements and does not set out optimum living conditions for the animals.

With meat production or laboratory animals, restrictive or experimental conditions are enforced. This is not the case when keeping rabbits as pets. With animals which have been entrusted to us for many years, it is vitally important to do more than minimum requirements demand.

The author reminds people who are keeping, or would like to keep, rabbits that they have a responsibility. Ruth Morgenegg would like to make them aware of the rabbit as a living being and its essential needs. I hope this book appeals to a broad readership and helps many animals to their basic rights and, with that, to better living conditions.

> Andreas Steiger
> Professor for Animal Husbandry and Animal Protection of the Veterinary Medical Faculty of Bern University.

How my passion for rabbits began

Many years ago in our veterinary practice, I received an unusual payment in kind – a lively, velvety-soft rabbit. I was taken by surprise and had no former experience of keeping rabbits. Therefore, at the beginning, the story of my rabbit was the same tale of woe as thousands of others – it lived alone in a small cage.

Soon, however, I discovered that, despite much attention and care, my rabbit was very lonely, so I decided to let it have a guinea pig for company, as many do. I did not know any better at that time.

The more intense my relationship became with the animals that were entrusted to me, the more I realised that this companionship between rabbit and guinea pig was not the solution. They got on well and seemed to understand each other, but a certain something was missing.

This is not the way rabbits should be kept. The cage is too small and a suitable environment cannot be created.

The next step was the building of an outside run, which allowed space for each animal to have a companion of its own kind. The result really surprised and pleased me, and awoke a passion in me for these animals. I watched their lively antics, their joy in running around and their companionship. Each animal now had a partner which understood its language. Finally, my rabbit was no longer lonely. From that point on I knew I wanted to devote my time to helping these animals in a special way.

However, I realised that keeping my rabbits in the most appropriate way was not that simple. The animals dug their way out underneath the fence or jumped over it and would not let me catch them in the evening, to mention just a few of the problems I was confronted with. I was enormously discouraged at the beginning, and trying to find any literature that could help me proved fruitless, so I had to learn from my own experience, step-by-step.

This was all a long time ago. The Rabbit and Rodent Refuge was then founded and over the years we have homed and brought together hundreds of rabbits. There is, however, still little knowledge amongst the public regarding the real needs of rabbits. Unfortunately, views like: 'rabbits are loners', 'they are sweet little cuddly animals' or 'they belong in a rabbit hutch', are still very widely held. In reality, rabbits are group animals which like to behave like wild animals and need a fair amount of space. These animals' basic needs are very often not recognised and therefore the animals pay with a life spent in dire circumstances. It is our desire to change this and work in the interest of the animals.

Education is a necessity. We have received thousands of calls in the past few years and many questions and problems were put to us. The huge number of rabbits that have ended up in our practice speaks for itself. Most illnesses and behavioural problems are no doubt due to inappropriate care and feeding, but it does not have to stay this way. The more the public knows about the principles of essential rabbit care, the greater the chance that prejudice will be questioned and errors corrected. With the help of this book, we would like to make as many people as possible aware of the needs rabbits have.

The following recommendations are based on the experience and knowledge we have acquired in our veterinary practice, Rabbit and Rodent Refuge, and through the Rabbit and Rodent Helpline over the years. This book focuses on the welfare of pet rabbits, does not consider commercial breeding and avoids any reference to breeds.

Dwarf rabbits are rabbits too

Dwarf rabbits have been bred and sold for more than one hundred years. Over this time owners have developed the attitude that dwarf rabbits are a different species from rabbits; that they are small, furry animals that have no special needs and are happy to sit in their cage looking forward to being stroked or cuddled.

What a rude awakening, though, when this little darling suddenly starts to rebel by tapping on the ground, chewing the cage, biting and scratching. This is when owners suddenly realise that dwarf rabbits are the same as rabbits - not just in some ways, but in every way, from the tops of their ears to the tips of their tails. Like their larger cousins, they have descended from wild rabbits and have the same characteristics and basic needs. They love company and enjoy running around, jumping and darting, nibbling on branches and digging holes. Once you realise this, you cannot help but wonder about the fate of the numerous dwarf rabbits that live in small cages and sometimes only serve as an extra ornament in a room.

> Dwarf rabbits are not specially bred animals without needs, but real rabbits that behave exactly like the larger species.

The breeding and sale of the dwarf rabbit has developed into a commercially orientated market in which the welfare of the animal is of very little importance. Dwarf rabbits are bred to be as small and as extreme in appearance as possible, which can cause health problems. They are often sold when they are far too young, in order to make them especially sweet and attractive to the spontaneous buyer. Who could resist such a sweet little thing that looks at you with big eyes? For the physical and psychological development of the animal, it should remain with its family for at least ten weeks after birth.

The animals sold as young dwarf rabbits are very often a larger species and grow to about six times their size in a very short time.

Small cages sold in pet shops might appear to be sufficient for a baby rabbit to begin with. However, within a few weeks they become far too small. This fact is often not mentioned. Instead you are given advice such as: "It would be best to have just one rabbit, give it a fair amount of attention and let it hop around outside the cage occasionally". The fact that rabbits are only happy when they are amongst other rabbits is often ignored. No human or other animal, such as a guinea pig, can take the place of another rabbit. It is also often forgotten that rabbits need space to exercise, otherwise their muscles weaken and they develop behavioural problems.

Dwarf rabbits have the same disposition and needs as large rabbits.

Dwarf rabbits are rabbits too

Besides their size, dwarf rabbits are no different from the stronger, larger species weighing several kilos. People like to see them as something they are not, and the rabbit and its needs are misunderstood or ignored. Everything that is mentioned in the following pages regarding rabbits and their care is, without exception, also appropriate for dwarf rabbits.

1 A short journey into the world of wild rabbits

If we are to understand rabbits, it is best to look at how they live in the wild. There is much to observe and learn from the wild rabbit and you will see many similarities in our domesticated animals, as all our pet rabbits are descended from wild rabbits.

Wild rabbits were originally inhabitants of South West Europe but there are also a few living in some regions of most European countries. Being extremely social animals, they live within a strong hierarchy. Several families join together and form a colony.

With enormous energy, the animals dig long burrows with several entrances and exits, as well as a living chamber. The mother rabbit creates a special place before giving birth. This chamber is padded with hair and, when finished, she gives birth to between 4 and 12 babies. She feeds the infants once a day and afterwards always shuts the chamber so they cannot be detected and so have optimal protection.

When the rabbit is startled, it taps the ground with its hind legs and this signal warns fellow rabbits of danger. They immediately all disappear into their burrows – rabbits can run very fast for short distances. There are many dangers from their natural enemies like buzzards, hawks, foxes, stoats and weasels. The large losses of the rabbit population are compensated for by intensive breeding. If there were no natural enemies, the prolific reproduction could lead to destruction of crops, and rabbits would become a plague.

Wild rabbits have specific colouring, which is called 'wild' colour. Their back is grey-brown, the stomach light grey-white and the underside of their tail is brilliant white. The animals are small and only weigh 1-2 kg. Zoologically they are classed differently than one would expect. They do not belong to the rodent family, despite having constantly growing gnawing teeth and the fact that their build, way of living and behaviour are very rodent-like.

1 A short journey into the world of wild rabbits

Rabbits are not hares and therefore not loners.

Also, although they resemble hares, they must not be mistaken for them.

■ *"This little hare is a typical loner, you can keep it very well on its own", says the sales assistant.*

Rabbits and hares are not related to each other and are very different in many ways.

Their habitat and way of living are also very different. Rabbits love company, but hares are loners even though they mostly live in pairs. The fact that hares are not group animals is often used as justification to keep rabbits on their own. If in danger, rabbits disappear in their burrows but hares run away. Baby rabbits stay in their nest for a while, as they are born naked, blind and deaf, needing protection for quite some time, unlike young hares, which leave the nest quite quickly. Hares are born with fur, the same as guinea pigs, and can see and move around immediately after they are born. They become independent very quickly. Hares and rabbits cannot interbreed.

> **Rabbits and hares are not related and are very different from each other. Unlike hares, rabbits live in colonies and are very social animals.**

The various types of rabbit are all descendants of wild rabbits. There are no hares that can be kept as pets. All the animals available for sale are, without exception, domesticated rabbits.

2 Species-appropriate care should be more than just a statement

Appropriate animal care is a concept that is a part of our modern vocabulary. Despite the fact that the care of animals and our ethical responsibility towards them is becoming more important, we should not become over-optimistic. Just because the words 'appropriate care' are on everyone's mind and are mentioned widely does not make the concept a reality.

The basic conflict between commercial and animal protection interests will never be solved completely. This is also true when looking after rabbits as pets. Much is known of their character, behaviour and needs, but what is lacking is putting this knowledge into practice when deciding on the choice and building of their habitat. As appropriate care for rabbits is more demanding, time-consuming and expensive than conventional cage-keeping, it is difficult to change people's way of thinking (and acting). When pet owners are not prepared to put more effort and cost into care, then the words 'appropriate care' are just that – words.

In this book we are trying to show forms of correct care for rabbits and dwarf rabbits that do not just concern practical questions like 'what, where, how or why'. Correct care requires thought, deed and emotion. Knowledge is necessary, but just as important is our relationship with the animal, intuition and two skilful hands. Appropriate care is demanding.

Rabbits can live for up to ten years. It is not easy to maintain the necessary motivation for the reliable care of our animals over such a long time. The easiest way to achieve this is to try and gain a sensitive and respectful attitude towards nature. Through this we will realise what kind of responsibility we have taken on with the domestication of these animals. We have removed these animals from their natural habitat and therefore made them totally dependent on us.

With good care, even a domesticated rabbit can become climatically adjusted and enjoy the snow. Photo: E. Hunziker

■ *"I am sure we are caring for our Benny correctly. We play with him and let him hop around in our living room."*

In the wild, rabbits occupy themselves with activities necessary to survival – building colonies, digging burrows, fighting to establish hierarchy, looking for food, breeding, rearing their young ones, etc. A rabbit which sits alone in its small cage can do none of this and is sentenced to deadly boredom. Nothing changes this boredom, even if we do spend an hour a day playing with it or letting it hop around in the living room – they are still alone for 23 hours.

Rabbits that are kept as pets are totally dependent on their owners. They have no possibility of changing their situation. The responsibility for their welfare is entirely ours. Our duty is to create a piece of their natural habitat and make sure they are kept in pairs or groups. This will make it possible for them to occupy themselves with exercising, digging, gnawing and socialising.

> To care for rabbits correctly, we need to look at their natural habitat and try to recreate this.

When appropriately caring for these animals, they need to be able to live according to their genetic predisposition. Only the care that makes this possible deserves the description 'appropriate caring'. Just saying the words is not enough.

By paying a great deal of attention towards the needs of rabbits, appropriate care is possible.

2 Species-appropriate care should be more than just a statement

An overview of rabbits' basic needs

- Social contact with other rabbits → Never keep just one rabbit
- Exercise → Large living quarters
- Gnawing → Natural gnawing material
- Digging → Natural ground
- Hiding places → Hutches and shelters
- Overview → Elevated areas
- Stimulation → Changing positions of hutches, branches etc. in the run
- Resting time → Being careful to give them time alone

3 The basic needs of rabbits

When we hear the words, 'basic needs', we immediately think of shelter, food and sleep. Animals, like humans, need a fulfilled life that is about more than just surviving. They must have the possibility to develop according to their disposition. Those who endeavour to offer their rabbits an appropriate life must know their basic needs.

The necessary knowledge is not acquired by sitting at a desk but rather through conscious and careful observation and intuition. The questions are very simple: what do the animals do all day long when their living area allows them to do what they want? How do they pass the time? What do they do often, rarely or never?

We have observed and compared a large number of rabbits over the years and have discovered that they are all very different in character and temperament. If they live in a large outdoor run, rabbits show a variety of behaviour which gives us an idea of their way of living and basic needs. It becomes clear that the behaviour of our pet rabbits is widely comparable to their cousins in the wild. If we want to care for our rabbits correctly, we should become familiar with how wild rabbits live.

Rabbits are group animals

Rabbits live in large groups. They are very sociable animals, which live in a social structure and are very conscious of each other. It is very important for them to know who is at the top and who is at the bottom of the hierarchy. Each animal has its place in the group. Either two animals like each other and show it in various ways, or they are sceptical or hostile, which is also clearly recognisable. However, they are never indifferent towards each other (see chapter 9, The unique social behaviour).

3 The basic needs of rabbits

■ *"Our Hoppy is one of the family," explains Mrs D. "I am sure he lacks for nothing."*

Company is very important for every rabbit. An animal kept on its own certainly suffers, even if many people refuse to believe this. In this regard there must be no compromise. Rabbits should never be cared for on their own, regardless of their living area. A rabbit living on its own cannot be considered as being appropriately kept. It is important to know that only another rabbit can satisfy its need for company. No human or other animal (such as a guinea pig, which is often mistakenly thought to be the ideal partner for a rabbit) can take its place. Each of these animals has its own ways and pattern of behaviour, which can only be understood by a member of the same species.

Rabbits need intensive social contact with each other.

It is possible for a rabbit to live peacefully with a member of another species or a human, but this will not give it the social contact it needs for healthy development and well-being.

> **A rabbit kept on its own suffers. Neither humans nor guinea pigs can give it the vital social contact it needs.**

The joy of exercise

Anyone who has the opportunity to watch rabbits with access to an area of a few square metres will realise how happy they are. It is something very special. Rabbits do not just walk when they move: they jump, dart, hop and demonstrate a whole series of different movements. They do not always try to achieve a purpose, often it is simply an expression of the joy of living and the pleasure of exercising.

> **Rabbits love moving. In a small cage their muscles weaken.**

Rabbits have extremely strong hind legs. A fair amount of strength is required to hold or lift a grown rabbit when it resists with its hind legs. It is also amazing how high they can jump from a standing position. They achieve this without any effort. When it can move around regularly it

Rabbits have a very strong urge to exercise, which can only be satisfied if they have enough room.

develops very strong muscles, but if a rabbit spends its days sitting in a small cage, its muscles deteriorate. For this reason it is absolutely incorrect to keep a rabbit in a small cage.

Rabbits gnaw, even though they are not rodents

Their continuously-growing teeth must be worn down and gnawing is a vitally important occupation to keep their teeth healthy.

Zoologically, rabbits do not belong to rodents, but their urge to gnaw is comparable. This specific gnawing behaviour is inborn and vital because their teeth, like our nails, constantly grow and need to be worn down. It is up to us to supply the animal with natural items from forests or woods and gardens to enable them to satisfy this need (eg various pieces of wood, branches, bark or roots). The rabbits will gnaw on these items with enthusiasm and occupy much of their time with this.

> Rabbits need natural gnawing material from forests or woods and gardens. Bread is not appropriate for this purpose.

Digging is more than just a pastime

If rabbits live on natural ground, they begin digging holes with their front paws, even before they are fully grown. Whilst digging, they make their run look untidy, change the ground structure and suddenly appear again, all dirty. Mounds will appear where before the earth was flat. Starting with the digging of a hole, this suddenly becomes a real burrow, which can be so deep that the end cannot be reached with your outstretched arm.

This is completely normal. Male rabbits do it, but it is predominantly females that dig burrows. The instinct to dig has been in rabbits from the beginning of time. The animals dig not just to pass the time, but to create something for survival, because in the wild they build their homes that way. This protects them from the weather and their natural enemies. Females dig special burrows where they give birth and bring up their young ones. This is the reason why rabbits have to be able to dig. The same goes for dwarf rabbits, despite the view that in this they are different than bigger rabbits.

Even domesticated rabbits want to dig.

> **Dwarf rabbits also dig because, as with any other rabbit, it is an essential occupation.**

These days our pets do not really have to dig, as they have been provided with hutches. But by instinct, despite providing them with artificial runs, they still demonstrate their natural behaviour, whether it makes sense or not. If they cannot find any soil, they dig around in the hay or tear up the newspapers we so carefully place in their cage. This fact cannot be changed: rabbits dig, cocks crow.

Rabbits are cave-dwellers in need of protection

In the wild, as mentioned previously, it is essential for rabbits to dig burrows to protect themselves from their natural enemies. They are only safe from an attack if they can quickly dart into their burrows. The burrows branch out widely and have several entrances and exits. This improves their safety, as it means there are several escape routes.

Our domesticated rabbits remain burrow animals, needing to retreat to protected places like hutches, a behaviour which is anchored deep in their character. A lack of such hiding places causes them a lot of stress. Despite the fact that they can live in any climate, which allows them to cope with low temperatures as well as rain or snow, they do need some dry areas where they can retreat to.

> Rabbits need a hutch which provides them with a dry and protective burrow, as well as many other retreats where they can feel safe.

A good panorama is also important

Rabbits not only retreat to safe places, they also love to be on elevated areas like the roof of their hutch or an uncovered higher area. Tree trunks and crates placed on their sides are also favourite places. The important factor is that the view is good and it provides an overview of the run. Rabbits love to be in such places, especially if they feel safe in their run. On these elevated areas they will stand upright, which is a typical pose for them, because it allows them to have an even better view.

Rabbits love to be on elevated areas.

Stimulation and change instead of boredom

Our pets do not have to fight for survival like rabbits in the wild. Their life is much calmer, different and can become boring very quickly. Their food is in the corner and everything smells familiar. Even in a big run there is the danger of boredom and you can imagine how much more this is the case in a small cage! Boredom causes stress. It can be a long day for a rabbit, despite the time we spend with them. That may sound trivial but it is often forgotten.

It is therefore important to know that rabbits need change and stimulation and, as they cannot organise this themselves, it is our responsibility to ensure that they receive it. To achieve this, we need to use our imagination.

> Boredom causes stress. Our imagination is required, as rabbits need much variety and stimulation.

Resting time is also part of it

Eating, socialising, exercising, gnawing, digging, keeping an overview and looking for variety: all these are basic needs for rabbits. But as they are so busy, there is also a need for rest, which they enjoy. For long periods of time they remain in the same place, half asleep and yet always alert, to avoid missing anything. They prefer resting places which give them an overview and offer protection.

Sometimes rabbits have their siestas lying on their side with all four legs stretched out, or fully stretched out on their stomach, especially in sunny and dry weather. At times they sit in the open to rest, as long as there is a place of safety nearby.

3 The basic needs of rabbits

Even the shade of a rock is a good resting place. Photo: S. Kurz/T. Dietrich

It is important to respect their time of rest. Rabbits do not run around on command and if we disturb them whenever we feel like it, we do them no favours.

Ignoring basic needs

There is probably no other household pet whose basic needs are so ignored as with rabbits. The main problem comes from keeping a single rabbit in a cage which is far too small. Such conditions are not appropriate and can lead to illnesses or behavioural problems. Appropriate caring can only be achieved when the animals are provided with their basic needs on a daily basis. The purpose of this book is to show how this can be done.

Happy rabbits

There has been much talk about being as happy as a lark, but not many people refer to happy rabbits. We would like to do this here by speaking up for these animals, which have been entrusted to us in the thousands to be provided for with an appropriate life. It makes us wonder how people who are so concerned with the welfare of farm animals can then keep their own pets in such an inappropriate way. There may be many reasons for this, one of which is surely a lack of knowledge regarding the basic needs of these animals. We are trying to rectify this lack of knowledge through education, and we would also like to point out that providing an outdoor run does not just benefit our pets, but also gives us, as owners, a lot of satisfaction.

4 Living outdoors – close to nature

The keeping of rabbits outdoors can be an enriching experience for the animals and for us, and can become a fascinating adventure over many years. To satisfy the needs of rabbits and dwarf rabbits, it is best to create a run similar to their natural habitat. A piece of garden is very useful for this purpose. Rabbits which are kept in a group in a run behave very naturally and they show their well-being by hopping, darting, hiding and digging burrows, which are cool in summer and warm in winter. They demonstrate an intense social behaviour. Sun, rain, wind and snow do not harm these animals if kept properly – quite the opposite, they seem to enjoy it. Anyone who has experienced this could not imagine keeping their animals any other way, because the outdoor life is not just the correct way to keep rabbits - the joy of living they express in such conditions can be deeply infectious for us humans.

> Caring for rabbits outdoors allows us to provide appropriate living conditions for these animals.

A few thoughts to begin with

Keeping rabbits outdoors can be rewarding but demands a certain amount of effort on our part. Before planning the run we should consider the following points:

Sufficient time. Feeding and observing the animals, as well as cleaning, creating and maintaining the run, demand a lot of time. You could easily spend an hour a day on them, and as rabbits can live up to ten years, we must understand that we are taking on a commitment for a long time.

4 Living outdoors – close to nature

Keeping rabbits correctly outdoors gives them and us a better quality of life.

Weather conditions. When poor weather conditions are predominant, as in northern Europe, it is essential to care well for the animals and ensure that the run is cleaned carefully on a regular basis. The worse the weather, the more important the care.

Hard work. In wet conditions, the appropriate maintenance of the run can be a messy job.

Costs. Correct care for rabbits requires a run of at least 6 square metres for 2 to 3 animals and costs a considerable amount. To economise when creating the run is not a good idea, as it will be exposed to all kinds of weather over many years.

Safe and practical run. Keeping rabbits outdoors requires a certain type of run. It must be safe and, above all, practical. To enjoy the run and rabbits for many years, it is extremely important that the daily tasks can be performed with ease, so that they will not become chores. Runs which are complicated and difficult to handle soon take away the fun and joy of it all.

The outdoor run

To keep rabbits outside all year demands a stable and safe run in which the animals can move freely at all times. It must be constructed so that we do not have to lock the rabbits away in a hutch at night, as they are also very active during this period.

A run which has proved itself must be:

- near the house, and with an overview from the house
- easily accessible (allowing the carer to stand upright in it)
- covered and with some kind of wall or fence dug down in the ground all the way around the run (it must be break-in- and escape-proof)
- practical to use (no complicated creations)
- for 2 to 3 animals, at least 6 square metres in size

(see chapter 5, The rabbit run – planning and building suggestions)

> Outdoor care requires a run which is stable, large and, above all, one that is practical for care and maintenance, so that it is a pleasure for all concerned.

Extreme weather conditions

Rabbits cope very well with all weather conditions in our part of the world. When an outdoor run fulfils the requirements laid out in this chapter and is created according to the needs of the animals, they can cope with heat as well as cold. Of course there are times when temperatures in summer or winter are extreme, but this does not require anything more from the owner than increased carefulness and thoughtfulness in designing and arranging the parts of the run.

For protection from heat and rain, the run should have a fair number of airy and dry places in the shade, in addition to the hutch.

Intense heat. Hot weather and intense sunshine should never induce us to cover the run or even close off their burrows to make it more comfortable for the animals. We would actually achieve quite the opposite: the heat would intensify and could easily cause heatstroke. On hot days it is essential to give the animals sufficient fresh water and plenty of shady places (eg roots, hollow tree trunks covered with branches and sprayed with water). We should observe the animals carefully, in order to detect if any of them have heatstroke. During high temperatures it is important to thoroughly clean their runs to prevent smells and swarms of flies.

> During high temperatures the rabbits are even more dependent on cool, shady areas, fresh water and good hygiene in their runs.

Long periods of rain. Sometimes it rains and rains and does not want to stop. In such conditions we should spread straw or hay thickly on the ground in the covered areas. If the run is in the shape of a pyramid, it is easy to cover part of it with plastic sheeting.

Extreme cold. There is normally no need to provide anything further if temperatures are low. It is, however, important that the covering and cleaning are done carefully and more often. We predominantly use newspapers, which help with the insulation, and also use plenty of hay. In winter there should be lots of hay in the hutches, the outdoor areas and the hiding places, so that the rabbits can sit in a dry place. If you use your intuition, you will soon know what to do and when to do it.

Heavy snow. Rabbits are not helpless in snow. They hop and dig around and are a pleasure to watch. The snow on the roof of the run should be removed, otherwise it can become dark underneath or the weight of the snow can cause the roof to collapse. The removal of snow in the run is only necessary as far as making sure that the hideouts, the hutch and the feeding areas are easy accessible for the animals and carers. If the snow is left in a heap, the rabbits will surely enjoy it.

> When it is cold, rainy or snowy, the rabbits need many dry places which are well covered with hay.

Extra areas for the rabbits to roam in as an alternative to the run

Maybe you own a big garden and say to yourself, "I will build an enormous run for my rabbits because I have so much room". That would be fantastic, but difficult to realise. However, there is a way to let the rabbits enjoy the whole garden, as long as it is blocked off against any roads and neighbouring gardens. During the night, the rabbits require a run of at least 6 square metres which is secure and does not allow either escape or entry. This makes it much easier to arrange for someone to care for them when we go on holiday, as they can then remain in the run while we are away.

Only in daytime. Of course such freedom and additional space can only be provided during daytime and is only advisable for grown animals. During the night, and for young animals, this is far too dangerous. If we shut the animals into a small rabbit hutch, assuming that they have now had plenty of exercise and will sleep deeply all night, we forget that rabbits doze and are actually active at night. Besides that, they do not like to be caught, especially when they know that they will be locked in a cage.

Even when it rains. In our part of the world we are well used to bad weather. We constantly hear, "We put the animals outside whenever it is a nice day.", but this means that the animals are probably spending more than half of the year in a small cage! Rabbits are not 'nice weather' animals. They have a strong instinct for exercise and cope well with rain, as long as they can occasionally disappear into a dry place. Not enough movement can lead to behavioural problems.

4 Living outdoors – close to nature

Even when they have an area where they can live freely, they need a run of a minimum of 6 square metres that is predator-proof and escape-proof.

Nightquarters. The activities of wild rabbits at night are very pronounced. At dusk they start looking for food, as the dark offers them more protection than daylight. Domesticated animals, kept in an outside run, will spend many night hours in the open, eat a fair amount and keep busy, even in winter when temperatures are low. Rabbits living in an outside run should therefore not be confined in a small area at night. They would become aggressive. It is important to keep a safe run of 6 square metres, or alternatively a shed that will enable the animals to move around freely. Besides that, the shed should also be accessible during daytime, so that they can eat, rest, or keep out of the rain. A shed should, however, never be used as the only quarters for rabbits, but rather only as nightquarters after they have enjoyed free movement outside in the daytime. Rabbits should be able to go outside even when the weather is bad or if it snows.

4 Living outdoors – close to nature

> Rabbits are not just nice-weather animals; they do not like to stay in the hutch in bad weather.

■ *"Our rabbits can hop around in the garden all day but it is a **real problem** to catch them in the evenings"*, says Mr M.

Punctual feeding in the evening. If you let your rabbits hop around in the garden all day, you will certainly wonder how you are going to entice them into their nightquarters, because they will not just walk into it like chickens which, when it gets dark, go straight to their coop. Catching rabbits is not easy, but luckily there is a way. Rabbits love a supper of dried grain and once you have got them used to it, they cannot wait for their food. If we give them their supper regularly at the same time, it becomes a ritual and they get used to it very quickly and happily hop into

Rabbits love, under supervision, to have the use of the whole garden.

their hutch. In winter, if we add a piece of hard bread to the grain, we will not even have to call them in anymore. To entice them into their hutch, their nightquarters must be comfortable and should not be cramped.

Effort required. The whole garden for rabbits would be wonderful, but it also requires that at least one member of the household is at home during the day. However, just using the garden area to avoid the effort of building a safe run is not acceptable, as the run is needed for night-time keeping anyway.

Misunderstandings about keeping rabbits outdoors

There are constant misunderstandings about keeping rabbits outdoors. There are pet owners who think keeping a rabbit outdoors all year means only putting a small cage on the balcony or in the garden. Keeping rabbits in small cages is never acceptable, and in a situation like this it could cause the animals to suffer greatly or even die, as they are exposed to heat, cold and dampness because they have no room to move about. They can suffer heatstroke and, when cold, have to try and keep their body temperature at a normal level by trembling, or they freeze to death. Conventional cages are always unsuitable, but outside or on a balcony they can become death traps.

> **A conventional cage never belongs outdoors. Many animals suffer greatly under these circumstances and can even die.**

We also do not consider housing rabbits in a traditional hutch as appropriate. These hutches are still used for animals kept for slaughter but cannot be considered to be the living quarters for pet rabbits that might live to an age of ten years.

> **Pet rabbits have a life expectancy of approximately ten years. Because of this, traditional rabbit hutches are not acceptable.**

There is one more misunderstanding. Contrary to what some people say, rabbits do not only become tame when kept inside. Gaining the trust of a rabbit does not depend on whether it lives inside or outside, but on how often and in which way we interact with it. Rabbits do not just enjoy contact with other rabbits, they also like contact with humans and therefore are easy to tame. However, this requires time, patience and a gentle approach, so that the animal does not feel cornered or frightened but is able to slowly gain confidence in us.

Finally, keeping rabbits outdoors must not be done only to get them out of the way. Those who keep their rabbits outside, just because they do not really want to be bothered with them, should not have rabbits as pets in the first place. Outdoor keeping is a form of care that requires a certain effort and is only advisable if we have an interest in the animal and are prepared to make the necessary personal effort. Inadequate and unhappy outdoor keeping results in great danger and risks for the animal and can cause the owner a lot of frustration.

> **Outdoor keeping must never be a way to keep rabbits out of the way. If we lack commitment, then this form of care is dangerous for the animals.**

Get rabbits – and keep them outside!

During our work and with this book we are specifically promoting species-appropriate keeping and caring for rabbits. For this reason, and in consideration of the animals' welfare, we would like to reiterate that rabbits should only be acquired if they can be kept in appropriate conditions, such as a large outdoor run. If this cannot be provided then it is better, in the interest of the animal, to avoid keeping rabbits and not to make poor or unsatisfactory compromises. Those who already own rabbits are encouraged to enter into the adventure of keeping their animals outdoors for their own and the animals' benefit.

We do, however, realise that many people who already keep rabbits are not prepared, or able for various reasons, to change but still want to keep their rabbits. This is the reason for chapter 7, Living indoors, where caring for animals indoors is introduced. Although this is not ideal, it goes part way towards the correct method of keeping rabbits.

5 The rabbit run – planning and building suggestions

■ *"We would love to keep rabbits. We have some garden and it should not take long to put up a fence."*

We may imagine that a run is easy to build, but in reality it takes careful consideration. Before we start to create an appropriate living area where the rabbits are protected, we need to clarify a few things. A fence around the run or a mobile run are unsuitable because they are neither exit- nor entry-proof.

Requirements for an outdoor run

Location:	Close by the house, easy to see
Size:	For two to three animals: at least 6 square metres, the bigger the better
Safety:	Break-in and escape-proof, meaning both covered and with a wall or fence under the earth
Maintenance:	Simple, easy to perform the daily tasks in it

Location

The location of the run is not a minor matter. We do not want to keep our animals out of the way by putting them in the corner of the garden. We would like to have the pleasure of watching them. An outdoor run should therefore be easily visible from the house and easily accessible, partly sunny with some areas in the shade, and visible from at least two sides.

And the neighbours: would they mind a rabbit run right next to their fence? What if, on a hot summer's day, despite your thorough cleaning, it still smells? Such questions can be easily resolved by a conversation with the neighbours. If the garden is part of a rented property, permission should be sought from the landlord regarding the building of the run, paying particular attention to the height of the construction.

Size

A run for two to three rabbits must be at least 6 square metres in size, and larger for more rabbits. The general rule is – the bigger the better. A run that is too small cannot be appropriately equipped. The animals would be unable to avoid each other and be restricted in their movements, which in winter is essential in order to maintain their body temperature.

Safety

Many novices start enthusiastically to fence in a section of garden, but that is not enough. Our rabbits will not be protected enough without certain safety measures in place. If we do not want any nasty surprises, the run must be protected from a break-in by predators such as foxes, and from an escape by the rabbits.

Escape Protection

Rabbits dig burrows of surprising dimensions, and, without appropriate safety measures, the exits of those burrows could one day be outside the run and the animals will be gone.

Break-in Protection

■ *"For years nothing happened, yet today they are all dead"*.

Rabbits are defenceless and easy prey for hunting animals. Having become tame and trusting, they no longer instinctively flee from their natural enemies. These enemies include:

- **Hunting birds** – They nose-dive from the air.

- **Ferrets, weasels, stoats** – They are good climbers and can squeeze through small holes and cracks. Use the marten test: wherever you can push an egg through, a grown marten will also get through.

- **Cats** – They sit there looking bored and suddenly grab a rabbit through the mesh of the fence. Surprisingly, a cat can kill a rabbit with one bite in the neck.

- **Foxes and badgers** – The tremendous strength and shrewdness of a fox is, unfortunately, grossly underestimated. A hungry fox can climb a fence of 2 metres or jump over a fence of 1.5 metres. It can kill a rabbit with its paw through mesh in a flash and easily bite through nets and thin wire fences. It can even dig under a fence and enter the run that way. A fox will not just come at night but also during the day, not just in the country but also in towns.

> Rabbits have many natural enemies. Only in a run with the appropriate safety measures can a rabbit be protected from them.

All these animals can be a danger to our rabbits. The many desperate phone calls we receive show us that the necessary safety measures are not always put in place.

When building outside runs, the following points are very important:

- The run must be covered with wire netting and not just soft nets.
- An extra underground fence must be put around the run, which should be dug in vertically to at least 500mm.
- The size of the mesh should ideally be 17mm, or a maximum of 40mm with the condition that the lower part is covered with an extra layer of smaller mesh.
- Moveable runs are never safe, as rabbits – and their enemies – can dig underneath.

Thin wire mesh fences or soft nets are not suitable, since predators can bite through them. We would also not advise laying a wire mesh on or under the ground in the run, as this will completely hinder the natural action of digging and can cause injuries by the rabbits' getting caught in the wire.

Digging the trench takes manpower. This trench is a very important part of the run.

Photo: J. Pfund

Easy handling

It is tempting to quickly knock together a run. But if it is badly planned and complicated to maintain, the work and the animals themselves soon become a burden. The care and maintenance in and around the run should be easy and not require that much effort, even when it is cold or raining, which is when our rabbits need extra care.

Height – As there are many jobs to do in the run, like cleaning out, spreading hay and feeding three times a day, the run should be high enough to allow you to walk upright.

Feeding house – If you install a well-made feeding house just outside the run, which is connected to the run by a pipe, it is easier to feed the animals, as you do not have to enter the run every time. You should be able to open the lid and lock it with one hand, as you never have enough hands when feeding.

Snow and leaves – When planning the run, it is important to think about how the snow will be removed, or if there is a tree near the run which will provide shade in summer but shed its leaves over the run in autumn.

> Important:
> Easy care and maintenance of the run is vitally important. If the daily jobs become a burden, the enjoyment of keeping rabbits is short-lived.

5 The rabbit run – planning and building suggestions

Choice of run

The following questions must be answered before choosing a run:

- How big should the ground area be?
- How high can it be built?
- Are there trees in the way? Low trees and bushes can be integrated into the run. The tree trunks should be protected with wire netting.
- How will the neighbours or the landlord react?
- How much will it cost? There should not be any economising with cheap materials.

There are three basic runs:

1. Pyramid run

This type of run has many advantages:

- It can be used as nightquarters or as a permanent habitat.
- The safety of the animals, as well as the necessary protected hiding places, can be easily realised.
- A platform can be fitted halfway up that allows the rabbits to have their beloved elevated place.
- A wind-free corner can be made by lining the far end of the run with wood planks or panels.
- The side walls can be covered with plexiglass or plastic to protect from wind, rain and snow.
- Leaves and snow slide down the side walls.
- It allows you to stand upright, which simplifies cleaning and feeding.

5 The rabbit run – planning and building suggestions

This pyramid-type run has many advantages. Photo: J. Pfund

2. High run with wire-mesh flat roof

It should be high enough for a grown person to stand upright.

Advantage:
You can walk around in it.

Disadvantage:
Leaves and snow lie on top of the roof and make the run dark. The roof needs to be cleared when this happens and there is also a danger of the roof collapsing. Protected areas – as in the pyramid run – are much harder to build.

This run is easy to walk around in, but leaves and snow on the roof can be a problem.

3. Run with open roof

Advantage: Size is not limited.

Disadvantage: The rabbits' enemies can climb over the fence, therefore it must have an electrified wire at the top.

When the run is so high that it cannot be covered, or if high trees prevent you from covering it, the following should be noted:

- The fence should be at least 2 metres high. A fox can jump 1.5m.

- If the top is protected with an electrified wire, it will keep out cats, ferrets, weasels, stoats and foxes.

- The habitat must have a good arrangement, with various hideouts, so that the animals can flee from birds of prey.

- A very large run would look like a cage if it was built with 17mm wire mesh. Suggestion: use 40mm wire mesh, which is marten-proof, and double-up with 17mm in the lower area, which will prevent cats from angling their paws in.

An open-top run is not limited in size, but must be equipped with an electric wire.

- To prevent a fox or badger digging in or a rabbit digging out, a gravel board or wire mesh fence of about 500mm can be dug into the ground. A concrete base is not suitable because then the water cannot drain off.

Threshold. A threshold approximately 300mm high, in the form of a horizontal board, should be fixed at the entrance to stop the animals from getting out when you enter the run.

The protected feeding area

In an outside run, a covered feeding area must be provided. It is a central area for the rabbits. Spreading fresh hay daily keeps the feeding area dry and also gives them some basic food. If that is where they clean themselves, then we should clean out the area daily. Apples, carrots and other fruits and vegetables can be given to them here. Juicy foods like dandelions, grass or lettuces should be served in a dish so that the hay does not get damp.

The sleeping den

A weatherproof hutch in any form of outside run is essential. It acts as a substitute for their natural burrows. Just like a burrow, the hutch must be airy, consist of several compartments and be big enough for the animals to rest in. It must be dry and protected from the wind and, most importantly, it must be dark. This way the animals feel safe and protected. The entrance must always be accessible.

When making such a sleeping den, the following should be observed:
- The hutch must be built of waterproof wood, which must be at least 20mm thick.

5 The rabbit run – planning and building suggestions

- The gabled roof should be covered with copper or a similar material.

- It is best to have at least three rooms, which gives the rabbits the option of avoidance if there is a conflict between the animals.

- When the size of the rooms has been established, they can be equipped with seed trays made of plastic, which will simplify cleaning.

- If the hutch is outside the run and connected with a concrete or clay pipe of approximately 200mm diameter, it allows easy access without having to enter the run.

- The hutch should have at least one side of the roof area open to reduce the heat in summer. There should also be at least four air-holes, depending on the number of animals.

- The pipe must never be shut off, as the animals could panic because of heat or lack of oxygen and, in a worst-case scenario, suffocate.

- The lid should be shut with a lock.

- The hinges should be fitted to allow the lid to be opened without any problems.

The hutch where rabbits sleep replaces their natural burrows.

5 The rabbit run – planning and building suggestions

Frequent mistakes when building a run

Height: Too low.

Electrified wire: Installed at 1200mm or below. A fox will easily jump over the fence without touching it.

Flat roof: Collapses under snow.

Wire mesh: Mesh size is too large. Foxes and cats can claw the rabbits and martens can break in.

Digging: The fence has not been put in deep enough and animals can dig underneath.

Break-in safety: This is not taken seriously enough. If animals are not locked in in the evening, they will be taken in the night. To try and catch the animals every night is not easy, in fact probably an illusion.

This run is no place for rabbits to live in: it is too low, too small and has no appropriate hutch.

5 The rabbit run – planning and building suggestions

Ideas for building a run

Photos:
B. Hiltl, R. Hafner,
M. Caplazi

5 The rabbit run – planning and building suggestions | 57

1. Safety

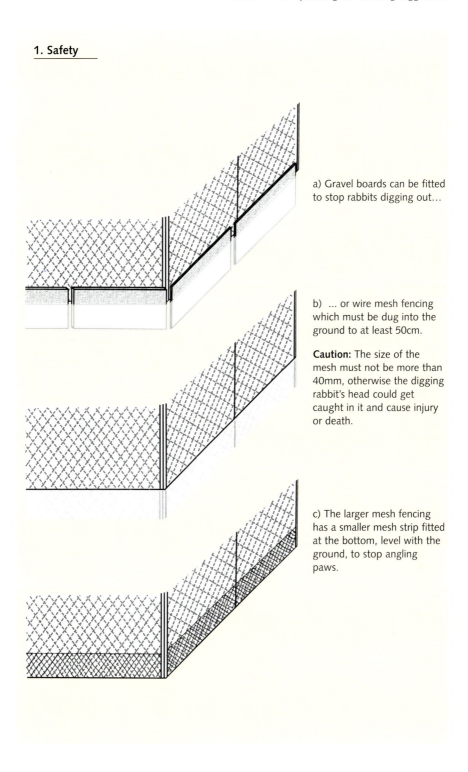

a) Gravel boards can be fitted to stop rabbits digging out…

b) … or wire mesh fencing which must be dug into the ground to at least 50cm.

Caution: The size of the mesh must not be more than 40mm, otherwise the digging rabbit's head could get caught in it and cause injury or death.

c) The larger mesh fencing has a smaller mesh strip fitted at the bottom, level with the ground, to stop angling paws.

2. Pyramid run

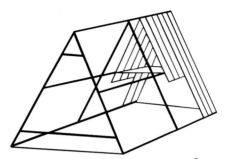

Assembly:
- Four side panels are singularly constructed.
- Connect two of each with hinges (1).

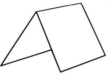

- Screw back panel to one pair of the side elements.
- Fit panelling boards at a higher level as a shelf. (2)
- Add second pair of side panels.
- Fit threshold.
- Fit door with hinges on left or right as the situation requires.
- Fix hasp and staple lock.
- Fit panelling boards as a protected roof area.   Short version: 1100mm
  Long version: 2000mm
- Cover apex with a panelling board.(3)

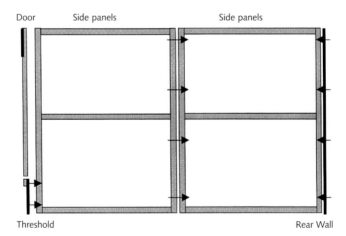

Tip: Accurate fitting is only possible if the ground is flat. Every variation in the ground level causes the run to shift.

5 The rabbit run – planning and building suggestions

Construction of the individual parts:

4 Panels:

Timber:
    (4.5 x 4.5cm):
    8 x 204 cm, 12 x 141 cm
Screws:
    24 x 9 cm (▶)
Wire mesh:
    8 x (145 x 100 cm),
    Size of mesh 17.5 mm
    Thickness of wire 1.5 mm
Hinges: 4
Staples:
    the wire mesh is fixed on the
    constructed elements (on the
    outside)

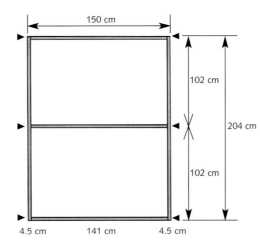

Rear Wall:

Weatherproof panel of at least 1cm thickness:
                      185 x 203 cm
Possibly 2 parts: 92.5 x 203 cm
                      92.5 x 106 cm
Screws: 8 x 4.5 cm

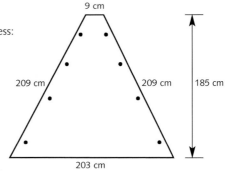

Threshold:

Timber (4.5x4.5cm):   1 x 171 cm
Weatherproof panel: 203 x   30 cm
Screws: 9 x 4.5 cm

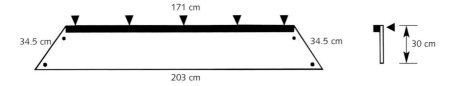

5 The rabbit run – planning and building suggestions

Door:

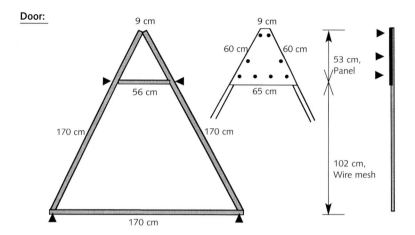

Timber (4.5x4.5cm)	3 x 170 cm	Screws:	4 x 9 cm
	1 x 56 cm		8 x 4,5 cm
Waterproof panel:	65 x 53 cm	Strong Hinges:	2
Wire mesh:	170 x 100 cm	Hasp & Staple:	1

Sleeping den

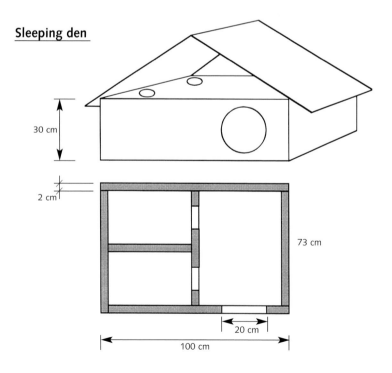

6 Creating and maintaining an outside run

■ *"Our rabbits have a house and a pipe that they can always hide in if they want to."*

If all goes well, our rabbits will spend many years in their run, so it is worth considering the installation carefully. The choice of its creative elements depends on the basic needs of the animals. We often notice that most animal lovers have no idea what the structure of an animal's living area should be and therefore create their runs wrongly. A hutch and a pipe are not enough.

A poorly-designed run.

A weatherproof hutch is necessary because the rabbits will want to retreat into a protective cave. Large alcoves, which are kept dry with lots of hay, are even more important because rabbits like to be outside, even when it rains.

> Having a large area for the living space is important but, more importantly, it should also be furnished correctly.

Furnishings

Some of the fittings should be moveable, which can then be changed as required, others should be in a fixed position. It is important not to place all of these items along the edges but to allow access all around them. This is especially useful when an animal has to be captured. Rabbits find out very quickly where they cannot be reached.

Overview of the most important fittings:

- weatherproof hutch
- covered feeding area
- elevated, protected area
- box or crate
- hollow tree trunk or pipe
- natural materials like branches, roots etc.
- earth mound or hazel bush

Weatherproof hutch

This hutch replaces the natural cave for the rabbits and should ideally consist of several compartments. It should always be dry and wind-protected inside. A double roof with an air gap will prevent overheating in the interior.

Traditional rabbit hutch - If a traditional rabbit hutch is used, at least one compartment must be protected from light and draught. This is easily done by covering the grid door with a wooden board. As extra insulation in winter, plenty of newspaper and hay should be used.

A weatherproof hutch with a good floor is a must.

A wooden board underneath. Rabbits prefer to dig their burrows in dry places (eg under a hutch or the food area). It is therefore advisable to put a board underneath so that if they decide to dig there, the hut does not tip. Such a board also protects against rising damp and can easily be replaced when rotten.

Never close the hutch. The entrance to the hutch must be open day and night. This ensures plenty of fresh air and allows the rabbit to leave the hutch when it wishes to do so. If the hutch is closed, it can become damp and lead to a lack of oxygen, which could suffocate the animals. It is not a good idea to lock the rabbits into the hutch, even if it is well ventilated. If they are confined in a small area, it can cause aggressive behaviour, and in winter lack of exercise can lead to hypothermia.

Placing the hutch outside the run. To gain space in the run, it might be useful to place a well-made hutch, which cannot be broken into, outside the run and connect it with a 200mm-diameter concrete or clay pipe.

To achieve this, a round hole needs to be cut into the fence. The disadvantage is that the area under the roof cannot be used by the rabbits. The advantage is that the rabbits can be fed without us having to enter the run.

It is much simpler to feed the rabbits if the hutch is outside the run, connected by a pipe.

Covered feeding area

Rabbits sometimes love sitting in the rain, but must be able to retreat into a dry area at all times. Food must be provided to them under cover. The animals love this area and often use it to clean themselves, as they tend to drop their excrement in places where they are fed. This is because they eat the special droppings (caecotrophs) which their appendixes produce during the night as soon as they make them. The 'normal' droppings are not eaten. This peculiarity is very important for the health of the rabbits and is connected with their special digestive system. With appropriate care and cleaning it is not a problem to use the same area for feeding and as a place for these droppings.

6 Creating and maintaining an outside run

A protected feeding area is vital.

A specially designated feeding hutch or the open roof area of the sleeping hutch can also be used as a protected feeding place. It is important, however, that it allows all animals plenty of space. It must have a wooden floor which can be covered with hay. A feeding area with a flat roof also provides an elevated space for them to use. It is best if this is close to the entrance of the run so it is easier to reach in the winter or when it is rainy.

Elevated protected area

If you provide your rabbits with an elevated sheltered area about a metre above ground and cover the floor with hay, you will soon find that it becomes the rabbits' favourite place. From there they can see what is going on all around the run and are protected from wind and weather. This viewpoint can be created by building a roof on the rabbit hutch or by covering the back part of the pyramid run and placing a shelf halfway up. Access is best provided by two wooden blocks.

Box or crate

Rabbits really enjoy having wooden boxes and crates of all shapes and sizes. These can be placed sideways to provide a hideout as well as an elevated area. The animals love these places. A crate or box padded with hay becomes a protected dwelling and its roof a viewpoint where rabbits will stay for a long time. With creativity and imagination, other fittings can be introduced. If you know your animals and relate to them, you will find all sorts of fixtures that they would enjoy.

> Elevated areas and protected hideouts are really appreciated by rabbits.

6 Creating and maintaining an outside run 67

The more hideouts, the better. They should also be clean and dry.

A hollow tree trunk or pipe

It is lovely for rabbits to crawl through something or hide themselves in a tunnel. They love and need dark hideouts into which they can retreat, as well as elevated viewpoints. As animals which cannot defend themselves against their attackers, they show strong escape reactions at the slightest noise or when an unusual object appears.

Natural materials

Rabbits love pine branches, various branches with leaves, thick pieces of wood and bark or roots. They enjoy nibbling and gnawing on them, climbing over and under them, quickly eating all the leaves, pushing broken pieces of the wood around etc.

Dwarf rabbits are also cave animals by nature.

There are three reasons why rabbits depend on regular replacement of fresh items from woods and gardens: they satisfy their need to gnaw, they constantly grind down their gnawing teeth, and it keeps them occupied.

Airy places in the shade. Large pine branches laid over a pipe or root make wonderful, shady places where the rabbits can rest when it is hot. Airy, covered places like that are very important in summer, offering a place for the rabbits to be protected from sunshine and intense heat.

Out of the woods. The regular collection of natural material from woods can be quite an effort. However, when we go for a walk, breathing in the wonderful, fresh air, collecting branches and twigs becomes a very relaxing experience. It might be useful to contact the forestry commission to obtain pine and other branches. At this stage it must be pointed out that thuja and yew are poisonous and must not be put in the run. However, if a small amount falls into the run, there is no need to panic, as rabbits which have been provided with plenty of gnawing material will avoid plants that harm them.

Natural materials such as branches are essential for a number of reasons.

Rabbits love mounds of soil to dig in and use them as a viewpoint.

Mounds of soil or hazel bush

Some additional things in the run will always be welcome. For example, rabbits enjoy a mound of soil to dig in or to sit on top of, with a good view all around. We could also plant a hazel bush nearby, which will provide shade and fresh branches. Just use your imagination!

Continuous change

A rabbit run should not be built and then stay the same forevermore. Even a large, well-equipped habitat becomes boring if nothing ever changes. So it is important that the pet owner considers what can be changed, added or replaced. The hutch and feeding area can stay where they are but it is more important where and how to arrange the daily fresh branches and twigs etc.

> We cannot offer rabbits the variety they have in the wild but we do have the opportunity to creatively change their living area so that they stay healthy and happy.

The most common mistakes when setting up a run

Hutch: The hutches generally available for guinea pigs and rabbits are not suitable for an outside run. They are too small, too light and not weatherproof.

Branches: They should not be left on the ground where they can easily get dirty or impede or injure the animals. It is much better to fix them onto the fence at some height or lay them across roots so the rabbits have to stretch up to reach them.

Cork and other pipes: These are only suitable for outside if they are large and heavy.

Ground: At least part of the ground should be covered with some absorbent material (eg hygienic bark bedding such as PetFix®), which should always be kept dry.

Structure: Often there are not enough fittings in the run or they are too small.

Cleaning jobs in the outdoor run

Part of the rabbit owner's job is mucking out. Cleanliness in the run, hutch and feeding area is important for the animals and for us. The animals have a very fine sense of smell and can be infested with parasites if they live in unhygienic conditions. Also, we will get annoyed if it smells or looks neglected. Cleanliness, however, does not mean "Mr Muscle" clean. We need a shovel, a broom, a rake and baskets to put the muck, and of course new hay, in. The plastic tray should be washed in hot water from time to time.

Cleaning the hutch

The sleeping hutch should be a soft, dry area for the rabbits. It needs to be cleaned at least twice a week, depending on the number of animals and how dirty it gets. When equipping the hutch, we should put newspapers on the wooden floor, and then a plastic tray covered with newspaper and hay. We recommend hay, as it is better than straw – or you can add a layer of hay on top of straw, as it is softer and warmer. Put a new layer of hay on top every day to keep it clean and dry. When mucking out, all the layers can be rolled up in the newspaper and removed very easily, then just sweep it up, refill and the clean 'cave' is ready.

The floor of the run

Not an evergreen lawn. We would love to provide an evergreen lawn for the rabbits but this is not realistic and also not necessary. Even if a fair amount of grass grows at the beginning, this will soon be trampled down or eaten.

6 Creating and maintaining an outside run

An overview of the most important fittings

It is our experience that it never grows properly again. The floor of the run – which should not be moveable as this would make it unsafe in terms of break-ins and escapes – will inevitably become earthy, sandy or muddy, depending on its texture and the amount of rain it is exposed to. A concrete floor should not be considered, as the water cannot then escape and the animals are deprived of their important digging.

Bark bedding: It is ideal if the ground of the outdoor run is covered with hygienic bark bedding (eg PetFix®) once a week or after heavy rain. This material is natural, absorbent and smells nice. The animals can move easily on it and the run always looks well cared for. It is easy to clean, as the dirty bark is raked together and replaced with fresh bark. Whether the animals always use the same area or leave their droppings everywhere will determine how often cleaning is necessary.

> The floor of the run should be swept once a week and covered with fresh bark bedding to prevent illness and infestation by parasites.

Different ground structures: To provide extra stimulation for the animals, you should use various floor surfaces such as slabs, gravel, leaves and bark. This also helps to keep their claws healthy.

Cleanliness in the feeding area

The feeding area is a place where rabbits often go and stay for some time, depending on the weather. Next to a heavy water dish, which should ideally be placed on a brick, there should be a hay rack and feeding dishes for fresh greens and grain.

6 Creating and maintaining an outside run

Eating and cleaning area. As rabbits like to defecate where they eat, we should make sure that the droppings do not end up in the food dish and the area is kept clean and dry. This is easily achieved if we cover the whole area with fresh hay every day. If the grain is soaked in urine or covered with droppings (this happens mainly with young animals, because they are so eager that they sometimes climb into the food dish), the dish should be washed and refilled. Weatherproof wooden planks are very suitable as a base for the feeding area because they can be easily cleaned. The feeding area should always be kept clean.

Absorbent bark bedding, stone slabs and a mound of soil make the best ground structure for rabbits.

7 Living indoors – when reality demands compromise

Not everyone who owns rabbits has the opportunity to keep them in the garden. Owners can, however, with the right knowledge and care, provide a dignified life indoors for their animals. There are various ways to keep them indoors, which would benefit all those rabbits which have not been cared for properly and which have perhaps even lived in a cage all alone.

Many rabbits are kept in the house and on balconies. Even without an outdoor run, many owners are prepared to improve living conditions for their animals and to do this we have to compromise. But we also have to make sure that we do not make cheap or bad compromises. In this chapter we describe how dwarf and other rabbits can be kept indoors appropriately.

Rabbits are group animals

With any type of rabbit care we have to respect the basic needs of the animals. Each rabbit needs at least one companion, as well as a habitat which allows it to follow its urge for movement. If you therefore own just one rabbit, it is imperative that you give it a partner. What kind of rabbit this should be, where it can be obtained and how the adjustment takes place are all questions that need to be asked, and you will find the answers in the following sections.

Guinea pigs are not enough

A guinea pig as a companion is not enough. Even if two animals of a different species live peacefully together, we are not being fair to either rabbit or guinea pig. Both of them have a completely different social behaviour and will still feel lonely, although not totally alone. Even human devotion cannot replace a companion from the same species.
(see chapter 13, Keeping rabbits and guinea pigs together).

Rabbits should be able to move, even in a flat, otherwise their muscles weaken and behavioural problems arise.

Unfortunately, people are often told to get a guinea pig as a companion for a rabbit because they fight less when living in a constricted area. Indeed, if two rabbits are placed in a conventional cage they often react aggressively, as they cannot avoid each other. Just imagine living with your partner in a bathroom – you can be sure it would end in a fight!

Cages and Animal Welfare Standards

Besides the need for a companion of the same species, exercise is another basic need which is just not possible in a conventional cage. Rabbits need to be able to jump, hop, run, dart and jump up on elevated areas. If this is not possible, their muscles will weaken and they become apathetic. Sitting behind the bars of the cage is like a prison. Often they suffer from obesity and become sick.

> The animals should be able to behave naturally in a flat. It is never enough to let the rabbits hop around in the flat for an hour or two a day.

Animal Welfare Legislation

The cages available in pet shops may comply with the rules and standards of your country, but in our opinion they contradict the basic principles of Animal Protection Laws set up in this book, meaning the animals should be kept according to the habits and needs of their species. Cages of this size do not allow the rabbits to jump, stand upright or dig. It is also not possible to keep them in groups. The authors of the Animal Protection regulations obviously were faced with an unsolvable problem to satisfy the demands from research, industry, livestock production, breeding and pet keeping. Unfortunately, the minimum size was determined according to the laboratory conditions. At the same time, the regulators have appealed to the common sense of the pet owners regarding keeping their animals appropriately and allowing them to behave naturally. The advice to keep to at least the minimum standards must not be used as an excuse to buy a small cage for the animals.

Our responsibility

The Animal Protection Law makes no differentiation between rabbits which:
- live for only half a year in a laboratory
- spend two to three weeks in a pet shop
- are fattened up for six months and then slaughtered for meat production
- are kept ten to twelve years as a family pet

7 Living indoors – when reality demands compromise

For the animals, however, it makes a lot of difference whether they spend six months or twelve years in a cage! Such cages are "recommended" to pet owners by the Animal Welfare Legislation, but this is based on only part of the law and has nothing to do with the words 'animal welfare'. The cages are not actually *recommended* by the legislation, but only satisfy the minimum requirements. This does not, therefore, release us from our own responsibility to take a critical look at the living conditions of our rabbits.

> **The Animal Protection Legislation makes no differentiation between laboratory, breeding, meat production and pet rabbits. It is our responsibility to give our treasured pets an appropriate habitat.**

Taking responsibility makes it possible for our rabbits to live a proper life.

Abnormal behaviour

Rabbits living in conventional cages or hutches with a fixed floor and firm walls or bars cannot behave naturally according to their genetic behaviour patterns. Massive behavioural problems can occur because of this, such as chewing the bars, constant scratching in a corner of the cage (an expression of stereotypical obsessive digging), or biting. The animals are actually screaming for help and showing us that they are not able to behave naturally.

> **Behavioural problems and stereotypical obsessive behaviour in rabbits are alarm signals which make us aware that we are not keeping them correctly. In conventional cages and hutches it is not possible to care for the rabbits properly.**

7 Living indoors – when reality demands compromise

Keeping rabbits indoors

The vivarium, which the rabbits can leave any time they want to, is an important part of their habitat.

If we are to take into consideration the rabbits' need for exercise, we have no option but to let them have a whole room at their disposal. This does not mean that the room concerned should be transformed into a giant cage without furniture, carpets and curtains and with straw on the floor. It should be a room where the rabbits can move freely, safely and feel comfortable but which can be used by us without too many restrictions. It is obvious that the nicest room with the Persian rug and antique furniture is not really suitable. Damage and small mishaps in the 'rabbit room' can be restricted, but never completely avoided.

The rabbit corner

One corner of the room should be established as the rabbit corner. There could, for example, be a vivarium, which can be 1.5m x 0.75m or something of similar dimensions. This is lined with newspapers, absorbent bark bedding and, on top of these, hay. The food is given to the rabbits in this area and for this we need a rack, a water dish placed elevated on a stone, as well as terracotta dishes for greenery and grain.

Fresh branches etc

Besides the food, a variety of gnawing materials will ensure that the rabbits happily visit the vivarium on a regular basis. Items such as branches, twigs and pieces of roots are very important for the well-being of the animals. They keep the rabbits occupied, keep their teeth healthy and satisfy their instinctive gnawing urge. We do not have to worry that we might bring in germs with these things. They do not create a problem for humans and they definitively improve the quality of life and immune systems of our rabbits.

A protective hutch

Although it does not rain in a flat and never gets bitterly cold, the rabbits need a protective hutch where they can retreat to and feel safe. The need to find a protective cave is deeply rooted in the animals. Of course, it does not need to be weatherproof, but it should be built solidly all the same and practical to deal with. The floor should be fitted with a plastic tray and lined with newspapers and hay. If the hutch has a flat roof, then it will serve as a favourite viewpoint. Ensure that other elevated areas can also be reached by the rabbits.

> Even if rabbits are kept indoors, they need a protective hutch so that they can retreat into the sheltering dark. Besides that, there should be various elevated areas easily accessible for the animals.

House training

Rabbits can be house-trained, but patience is required. As the animals mostly do their business where they eat, they eventually choose the vivarium as their toilet. To encourage them, it may be an idea to put some of the droppings in there or we could provide a separate box, covered in hay, collect the pellets and put them inside. If the rabbits choose another area as their toilet, then we just put the box there. We should observe our animals and with a little trial and error, and a lot of patience, we will eventually succeed in house-training them. Playful young rabbits will take a little longer.

■ *"Max and Mimi have always done their business in a box but since we got a new rabbit this does not work anymore"*, said Mr P.

If animals are new to each other, it means stress – and cleanliness will not be the first thing on their minds. Once they get used to each other it will improve and the same applies to the habitat: if it is new and strange it can take months to settle in. It is therefore worth being patient. The fact is, even house-trained rabbits sometimes mark their territory. It does not pay to be fussy when you keep rabbits indoors.

Gnawing is wonderful

Gnawing is a wonderful, important and useful occupation for rabbits, which should be made possible even if they are kept indoors. What interests us most is what they gnaw. When the legs of the chairs are bitten into or the fringes of carpets disappear, we do not find it funny anymore. If electric cables happen to get in between those busy gnawing teeth, it can become dangerous for the rabbits, as they can easily cause a short circuit and die of an electric shock.

There are only two solutions for unwanted gnawing. Number one – provide the animals with plenty of fresh gnawing material (eg pine branches, leaves and fruit tree branches, bark etc). Number two – the room should

7 Living indoors – when reality demands compromise

Natural fresh gnawing material should be provided on a daily basis even if rabbits are kept indoors.

be checked for possible danger and made safe. It is best to move that heirloom that you do not want to put at risk into another room and place or cover all electric cables so that the rabbits cannot get at them.

Keeping rabbits on a balcony

Rabbits can also be kept on a balcony, but only when it is not facing south. If it is facing south, it is not an appropriate area to keep rabbits, because long and intensive sunshine will make it too hot. This problem cannot be solved by rolling awnings out or hanging up sheets. Quite the opposite, such actions store the heat and make it completely unbearable. If you have a north-, west- or east-facing balcony, it may become a habitat for rabbits. But balconies must never be a way of getting rabbits out of the way.

With some imagination a balcony can become a good habitat for rabbits. Photo: J. Roshard

Exercise in large areas

When keeping rabbits on a balcony day and night, they should have an area of at least six square metres at their disposal. They must be able to leave their cage or hutch at any time. This way they are able to keep their normal body temperature level by moving around in the cold and keeping cool when it is hot by finding shady places.

Natural hideouts like roots, boxes or pipes are most important and if installed and maintained sensibly the balcony can still be used by everyone, including humans! For the protection of the animals you should fit the balcony with a strong mesh fence right up to the top, with holes that must not be too big. This way the rabbits are protected against predators, like martens and cats, and do not risk falling if they try to jump up onto the railing.

Even digging is now possible

As when keeping rabbits indoors, we can now use a corner of the balcony to provide them with a vivarium as a food and gnawing corner as well as a toilet. It is advisable to cover the balcony floor with leftover pieces of Astro-Turf for insulation, leaving part of the concrete exposed. Even on a balcony it should be possible for the rabbits to dig and for this purpose we should provide big plant pots or bowls filled with soil or sand. Of course, when rabbits dig they can spill some of the soil or sand but instead of getting angry, it is much better to enjoy their zest for life and the way they undertake these activities, which show that they are behaving normally.

Weatherproof hutch

It is obvious that if rabbits are kept on a balcony all year round, it is essential that they have a weatherproof hutch to provide them with protection from the wind, cold and damp – even if the balcony is covered. Conventional hutches, as used indoors, are never sufficient for outdoors. Rabbits need their cave to feel safe. All sorts of things can scare the rabbits, especially in the dark. The hutch should be open day and night because, as previously mentioned, rabbits are also active at night-time.

Do not forget neighbours

If you keep your rabbits on a balcony, it is important to tell your neighbours and to ask for understanding for any possible inconvenience. This can affect the neighbours' noses and ears.

7 Living indoors – when reality demands compromise

A weatherproof hutch is essential for any form of outdoor keeping.

Photo: J. Roshard

The odour of the rabbits, and their droppings and urine, can lead to an unmistakeable aroma, which can never be completely avoided, despite the daily cleaning that is absolutely essential for balcony keeping. When the weather is hot, it can start smelling very quickly.

If a rabbit is frightened by something, it starts tapping really hard against the floor with its hind legs. In the daytime no one would take any notice, but in the quiet of the night it can be very noisy and disturbing. It is important to have an informal talk with the neighbours before it becomes a problem.

Rabbits on balconies can often be smelt and heard. It is therefore important to have a good relationship with neighbours.

Spaying of females is recommended

Most pet owners are familiar with the fact that if you keep rabbits in groups, the male rabbits must be castrated to reduce extreme odours and avoid offspring. If rabbits are kept indoors, it can also be sensible to spay the females.

Heat and false pregnancy

Female rabbits, in heat every two weeks, do not always react in the same way. There are those whose behaviour can become unbearable, because they become highly active and try desperately to dig a cave to build their nest in. When kept outdoors, it is not really a problem. Indoors or on the balcony, overactive digging and scraping is undesirable and it can be disturbing if the animals pull out their fur and carry bundles of hay and straw through the room to build a nest. When female rabbits are in heat, they become bitchy and aggressive and can even bite. Neutered females are much quieter and calmer.

Female rabbits with repeated false pregnancies are best spayed.

Females that are not spayed often go through a false pregnancy. This is due to a hormonal problem which leads to the body simulating a pregnancy. The rabbits demonstrate the behaviour of a pregnant female and occupy themselves with digging and building a nest. Explicit information regarding the neutering of males and females can be found in chapter 10, Reproduction and Birth Control.

Uterus cancer

Up to approximately 80% of the females older than three years suffer from uterus cancer. This can be avoided by spaying young females.

Indoor places which are unsuitable habitats for rabbits

At first sight, a summer house, garage or cellar might appear to be a suitable residence for rabbits. However, this is not the case. These areas are often too far away from our daily life and make it difficult to keep the necessary contact with and control over our animals. Besides that, it can get very hot in a summer house or a garage with not enough fresh air. This lack of fresh air is especially the case in cellars, where it is also usually dark.

Keeping rabbits outdoors is the best method

Finally, to end this chapter, we would like to emphasise that with this book we would primarily like to promote outdoor keeping. Only with a large run outdoors can we reasonably satisfy their basic needs. Besides that, this type of keeping is a nice hobby which allows owners to enjoy caring for their rabbits over many years.

7 Living indoors – when reality demands compromise

■ *"I want to keep my darlings in my flat, as this way I can keep in better contact with them. I don't want to keep them out of the way."*

Even rabbits kept outdoors stay tame if we take the necessary time.

Basically, keeping rabbits in a flat should be discouraged. Even the best indoor care is in many ways insufficient, because the basic needs of the animals can only partly be satisfied and it can cause numerous problems. We would urge animal lovers who are considering getting rabbits to do so only if they can keep their animals in a species-appropriate way outdoors (see chapter 4, Living outdoors – close to nature).

> **Keeping rabbits outdoors should not be a method of keeping them out of the way, but rather a form of care which is much fairer to the animals.**

8 Acquiring your new rabbits

Each pet story starts with enthusiasm, interest in a new task, warm feelings towards the animal and many good intentions.

At the beginning everyone is enthusiastic

Children's hearts beat faster when they are near a sweet, furry animal. Everybody is happy: the children with the cuddly little rabbit and the parents with the joy of their children. There are so many promises and good intentions before the purchase. The new member of the family is not going to lack for anything. The rabbit is extensively stroked and cuddled. Every move is watched and commented on. The little guy receives a name and is the centre of attention without any competition. The children even fight over who will feed or clean out the rabbit's home. That is music to the parents' ears. So much goodwill and undiluted pleasure – this rabbit has hit the jackpot.

Who can resist such a bundle of fluff?

What is the next stage?

A few months later and the little darling has become quite an ordinary, and possibly an unexpectedly large, rabbit. The charm of the youngster has changed into the behaviour of a grown-up animal, which is not so cute anymore. Maybe the rabbit has adopted habits which we do not like at all.

The fights over who is allowed to feed and clean have now become battles over who **must** feed and clean. And who is going to let the animal out of the cage for a while and then catch it to put it back? Because of the penetrant odour, you are seriously considering moving the rabbit into the garden shed. You would make sure it was visited and fed daily and the cage cleaned now and then. As rabbits are, according to general literature, robust, frugal and undemanding, this move would surely be justified. And that is how this once idolised member of the family becomes a nuisance whose care is only attended to with minimum effort.

An animal is not a thing

Animals do not count as a 'things', according to Swiss laws at least, and quite rightly, because there is a certain way of dealing with 'things'. We acquire them, find pleasure in them, get fed up with them and eventually get rid of them. Unfortunately, there is a similarity to this in the way we deal with animals: quickly bought, swiftly loved, tolerated for a little while and finally given away and forgotten.

The number of homeless animals is constantly growing. In our throw-away society, animals have unfortunately become throw-away things. It is a sad fact that more than half of the rabbits which are kept in flats die prematurely, are given away, are abandoned or finish up in animal shelters even before a third of their life expectancy has been reached. This is especially sad when considering that rabbits can reach an age of eight to ten years.

> **Rabbits are, like all animals, precious creatures. They are loans from nature and have a right to live a dignified animal life.**

Enthusiasm which is not 'here today and gone tomorrow'

Fortunately, there are pet owners who make an honest effort to consider the needs of the rabbits and recognise they must be kept correctly, even if it means a little more effort. After the initial excitement, they try to intensify their relationship with the animals and have many rewarding experiences. It is especially important to consider things like the habitat, care, and who you are buying it from, before getting a rabbit.

No spontaneous purchases!

■ *"The two were just so sweet, I could not resist and have also bought the biggest cage available. No-one told me they would grow so large."*

This quote could come from someone who purchases rabbits:

- on a whim
- out of pity
- because the children insist
- because one of the children has his/her birthday
- because young rabbits are so sweet
- because someone else wants to get rid of the animals

These owners are often not in a position to create really good living conditions and to care for the rabbits for years.

> It is advantageous to seek advice from a competent person who has nothing to do with selling the animals.

When buying an animal, the advice given is often more in the interest of the business than the welfare of the animal. With a spontaneous purchase, the customer often buys animals and fixtures without much thought or research and is soon confronted with the first problem. You should, before any purchase, seek advice from an expert who is in no way connected with the sale of animals (eg Animal Welfare Society or one specialised in rabbits and rodents, if this exists where you live).

The sad result of a spontaneous purchase. Because the cage was too small, the rabbits attacked each other and were therefore separated with a piece of carpet placed in the middle of the cage.

Can rabbits be kept species-appropriately?

Before the acquisition, we should think about where the animals will live. In many pet shops there are still only conventional cages available. If one considers the varied needs of rabbits, one realises that they belong outside. A traditional cage is never a suitable habitat for such active animals. Any other commercially-based advice should not be believed and we urge anyone wanting to acquire rabbits to keep them outdoors.

> **Questions which should be asked before purchasing rabbits**
>
> - Is our garden big enough?
> - Can we install a run?
> - Who will build it or where can we get it?
> - Where will we keep all the items like straw, hay, fodder and cleaning utensils?
> - Can we financially afford to keep our rabbits outdoors?
> - Do we have enough time to care for the rabbits?

The necessary time and funding for the purchase of the animals, run, food, hay, as well as veterinary costs, must not be underestimated. The responsible action might be not to purchase any rabbits, despite your love of animals, the pestering of children and the sweet look of cuddly animal babies… because we simply cannot offer them appropriate living conditions!

Holiday care

Who will look after the rabbits when we are on holiday? There is considerably more work involved than in watering flowers or emptying the letter box. We should therefore find a person early on who is prepared to look after the animals responsibly and invest the necessary time. It is preferable to keep the rabbits in their usual environment. Putting them together with another group of rabbits should not be considered, as it takes too long for them to adjust and causes too much stress. Locking up the animals in a cage should not be considered either.

Buying because the children beg

Very often rabbits are purchased because it is what children desperately wish for. They have seen such a sweet little animal at a friend's house or in a pet shop. Those of us who know children, know how insistent they can be. Rabbits, or any animals for that matter, should never be bought mainly for children. Although they have waited a long time for the fulfilment of their wish, the enthusiasm is normally short-lived and good intentions are forgotten very quickly. Rarely does the pleasure last over years and this is because, at a young age, our interests change frequently and we want to learn and experience many different things. This is normal and has nothing to do with being irresponsible. There are always new things that occupy children's time, such as stress at school, friendships, leisure activities and the like. The result is frustrated parents being tired of constantly reminding children of their duties towards the neglected animals. Indifference and resignation lead to the rabbits being left more and more alone. They then become apathetic and very unhappy in their uncleaned cages or runs. Because they are so bored, they eat more than is good for them.

> **Buying rabbits for children is only sensible if at least one parent supports them with pleasure and responsibility.**

Rabbit care demands too much from children

The care of rabbits by children alone demands too much of them. A cat or a dog can let us know of their needs. Rabbits however, do not inform us when they are hungry or thirsty, when their hutch smells or when they are bored. They suffer quietly, resigned to their fate. To detect indisposition or illness early, one has to have some degree of knowledge and to observe the animals carefully. Children are not able to do that; only grown-ups can.

For this reason, one or both parents should take an interest in these animals and support the children in their care. Rabbits are not soft furry animals which can be stroked, cuddled and carried around whenever we feel like it. Unfortunately they are often treated like that and this can easily go wrong. Due to their delicate build, young animals should never be carried around by children. In our practice we often see animals which have slipped from children's hands and have broken bones. Although young and playful, the animal then has to be separated from its group to heal.

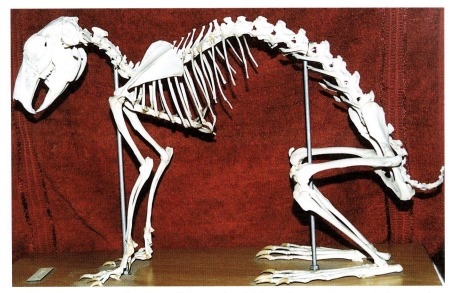

Rabbits have a very fragile build and should therefore not be carried around by children.

Rabbits do not always like all forms of attention. If they dislike something, they scratch and sometimes even bite. You should be prepared for that to avoid being hurt. Children and grown-ups often underestimate such sudden reactions. If we treat our rabbits properly (eg speak to them, stroke them without picking them up and feed them by hand) then they can become tame and will enjoy our attention.

The responsibility of parents

In the interest of the rabbits, parents must take responsibility for the animals' welfare. Their pleasure in this task is a very important condition for the purchase. Children can learn how to be a responsible pet owner from their parents. Under instruction and the control of an adult, children are capable and motivated to take on some of the main duties of animal care.

Rabbits can live for up to ten years. This means that, with every purchase, we take on a long-term commitment. Every day, and in every weather, even when we are not well, we have to care for these animals. Careful consideration before taking on such a project is therefore vital.

The keeping of rabbits, like any pet, gives us and our children the opportunity to get to know and understand the animals. There is always something new to discover, as each animal has its own character. Children who grow up with animals and help with their care learn consideration and intuition towards these creatures. As rabbits can become very trusting, a wonderful relationship, with a deep affection between animal and human, can develop. Acquiring rabbits can really enrich the lives of grown-ups and children.

If parents deal respectfully with the animals, the children will also be able to build a good relationship with them.

Photo: Ch. Ziörjen

Where do we acquire our rabbits?

This question deserves special attention, as there are various ways to obtain rabbits.

From an animal shelter

It is a sad fact that hundreds of rabbits, including young ones, end up in animal shelters. It is therefore well worth considering whether we can give such animals a nice, new home, and with that make a meaningful contribution to active animal protection. In a good animal shelter one can find rabbits which are neutered, vaccinated and used to each other. In this way the initial difficulties like medical care and nerve-wracking re-adjustment can be avoided.

Young animals are waiting in animal shelters for responsible animal lovers.

> The question of where our rabbits come from is not unimportant. Hundreds of rabbits are waiting in animal shelters for a good home for life.

From a breeder or pet shop

Breeders offer rabbits for sale directly or via pet shops. For health reasons, young animals should stay with their mother for at least ten weeks. Good pet shops should not sell babies, single animals or uncastrated males (unless they at least advise the buyer about early castration). Unfortunately, there are also some who sell the animals far too young, so that they look cute and fit neatly in small cages, and with that expose them to risks of illness. Customers who buy rabbits that are too young are jointly responsible with the sellers for such problems. When buying rabbits, such aspects should be brought up. What customers are not willing to accept will influence what is on offer. For the animals that are on offer, pity is not a good basis for purchase. So please do not let sad-looking button eyes tempt you.

Second-hand rabbits

Because rabbits breed so extensively, many young animals are passed on through acquaintances and newspaper ads. Hardly a week goes by without an advert in the free advertiser offering small dwarf or other surplus rabbits, often with a cage. The words 'free of charge' serve as bait and are meant to make the decision easy for the new owner. Something that is free can be sampled – and if it does not work then just pass it on. Basically, such free gifts are an expression of disrespect to the animals.

> If young rabbits are easy to pass on, this will increase uncontrolled breeding. But animals are not disposable things.

Whoever accepts a young animal second-hand should ensure that the baby has been with its mother for ten weeks and should also ask whether the father of the animal has been castrated. If he has not been castrated, then it will not be long before the next lot of babies needs to be placed. Through such careless action, many animals suffer. The demand for rabbits is there, but good homes are rare. The taking on of surplus rabbits is only then acceptable if, at the same time, the castration of the father is requested and carried out.

Taking on rabbits which have lived in poor conditions

■ *"The male rabbit lived for years with a guinea pig called Bob in a cage that was far too small. We have taken over both of them and built them a much larger enclosure."*

Of course we must not close our eyes when we can aid an animal, but our offer is only sensible when it really helps them. Small (and often insufficient) changes only serve to clear our conscience but do not consider the welfare of the rabbit. In the above case, it would be sensible to castrate both animals, add two females and house all four in an outdoor run. Pity is not a good basis for taking over animals that have been kept in poor conditions. It must also be remembered that re-housing an animal causes a lot of stress, and this should only be considered if the new place is guaranteed to be permanent and with a good habitat. If you find that you are not able to offer the rabbits an appropriate life, you can actively work for the welfare of the animals by finding a new, better-suited home for them.

Senseless breeds

Senseless breeds should not be supported. By this we mean breeds like extremely small animals that often have deficiencies such as the position of their teeth. They are very often much more aggressive than other members of the same species, so people who have some knowledge about rabbits often decide on a larger breed. Over-breeding leads to various problems: the fur of the mohair rabbit, for example, even if kept properly, gets knotted and matted very quickly. Such animals have to be anaesthetized to be shorn every three months. Or, for example, English Lops have such long ears that they are constantly injured because they keep standing on them.

Even though each animal basically has the same right to a dignified life, we, as purchasers, have to be aware that if we buy an animal from these extreme breeds, we increase the demand for such animals. Of course, this is not the same if such an animal is waiting in a refuge. We have nothing against such an adoption, because it does not further more senseless breeding by a shopkeeper or a breeder.

The problem of uncastrated males

In available literature, it is mostly recommended to get female rabbits. This is mainly for commercial reasons, because if a pair – or two males – were on offer, then there would be a need to point out that they should be neutered. If this had already been done, the price would be higher and therefore a customer might decide against a purchase. Males are often paired with guinea pigs. This, as mentioned previously, does not do justice to either animal and often leads to problems later on.

How many animals should we take on?

People who know that rabbits should not live alone normally get two. However, there are good reasons to take on at least three rabbits, such as:

- several animals stimulate each other to more active behaviour.
- if one rabbit dies, there is enough time to find a suitable new rabbit, as a group animal should never be kept on its own, not even temporarily.
- it is much easier to put together a group of rabbits in a new run. Once the animals have claimed their territory, a new animal cannot be integrated without hierarchy fights, which can be intense and last a long time.

A group of three to four animals develops normal social dynamics.

> If three or four rabbits are kept together, then their behaviour is much more lively. And if one dies, it does not have to be replaced immediately.

Information regarding the gender and integration of the animal can be found in the next section.

When the rabbits arrive

Finally, when everything has been thought of and the rabbits' place of origin has been decided, the impatience, especially of the children, starts growing. However, a good start should now be the basis for a long and good time with our animals. Therefore, it is important to proceed with prudence.

Getting their habitat ready

To introduce the rabbits to their new home as peacefully as possible, the run should be ready before the animals are bought. At the beginning, our darlings have to cope with a new environment and strange noises and are possibly together with other strange animals. The stress of adjusting (see next chapter) should not be increased by construction and other disruptions, as the rabbits can become very anxious or even aggressive.

Practice restraint

The children might approach the rabbits quite impetuously in their first excitement, but the rabbits do not like that. It can happen that they scratch or bite when being picked up or get hurt when falling. Excitement and carelessness can lead to disastrous accidents which can spoil the joy felt at the beginning.

The children do not like hearing it and grown-ups sometimes also find it difficult, but it is advisable to proceed slowly and carefully, being patient and showing consideration. "Look with your eyes and with not your hands." This way we give the children an example of considerate handling of our rabbits right from the start. This is a condition for creating a happy life between animal and human. Not just in the beginning but over many years.

9 The unique social behaviour

Rabbits are not loners. On the contrary, they are group animals with a specific need for social contact. It is very important for their welfare that they live with another rabbit – or rabbits. If a rabbit is kept on its own, it is deprived of exactly what makes its life worth living: that lively and varied exchange with animals of the same species.

Every rabbit needs companions of its own kind

■ *"My Bunny can run around in the garden all day, summer and winter; I am sure he lacks for nothing."*

This is the wrong interpretation. Bunny lacks a companion of its own kind that understands its behaviour and with whom it can have social contact. Neither a human nor an animal of a different species can be a proper partner for a rabbit. A rabbit can, of course, become very trusting with the person who looks after it, but this relationship with a human - or other animal - can never replace contact with another rabbit. Only by living with one or several other rabbits can it satisfy its need for social contact. If you want to keep your animals appropriately, you must realise that even the largest and most beautiful run cannot take away the loneliness and psychological suffering of the animal.

> A group animal should always be able to live with animals of the same species, otherwise behavioural problems will occur. Half a month of being kept on its own is equivalent to half a year's isolation for a human being.

A rabbit will only feel really happy and healthy if it has the company of at least one other rabbit.

Why are so many rabbits kept on their own?

Even though rabbits are group animals, they will start fighting if they have to live in a conventional cage. This is not because of adjustment problems, but because of the constant lack of space and something to do. We would react very similarly if we were locked up together with another person in a small room. Unfortunately, there are few pet shops which offer appropriate cages, so these animals are continually sold individually, or with a guinea pig, for commercial reasons. It is up to the consumer to consider this grave problem and act accordingly.

Social contact - different forms of behaviour

Life amongst rabbits is very similar to our own. They like each other and they show it, or they argue and they fight. After some difficulties they will get on together again or, for a while, avoid each other.

When we observe our rabbits, we will not just see exciting things but also many things that one rabbit does or likes or dislikes, and another does not. They are born with a variety of behaviours, but every animal will also develop its own individual peculiarities.

Intimacy. Rabbits greet one another by gently prodding each other with their snouts. They cuddle up and lick each other's head and ears with tremendous patience. This social grooming of their fur helps with hygiene, as rabbits are very clean creatures, but the main purpose is to establish friendly relations within their community and satisfy their great need for physical contact. A rabbit prods its partner with its snout and with that begs for affection. When enough caresses are exchanged, it will push the other rabbit away with its snout. If an animal does not want to be disturbed, it lets the other animal know with a harder snub with its nose.

This is not an act of mounting but an expression of social dominance – or just a gentle cuddle.

Movement. At times, the animals chase each other through the run and seem to play hide and seek. When tired, they like to retreat alone to rest. Something typical in rabbits is the mounting of companions of either gender. With this behaviour, which also has sexual components, they express dominance. Anyone observing this will wonder whether they actually have a female rabbit and not a male. Such doubts can only be dispelled by sexing by an expert.

Identification. Rabbits mark their territory and make themselves understood with the help of a scent which is produced in various glands (eg under the chin, in the groin, in the anus). They cover their droppings with the secretions from the anal glands and this, together with their urine, serves to mark their territory and enables them to recognise each other, thanks to their flexible and sensitive nostrils.

Tapping. A rabbit will express feelings like insecurity, fear or surprise by tapping hard on the ground with its hind legs. This is to impress the enemy and to warn other animals. Its whole body becomes tense, its ears flatten and its eyes widen. This tapping is a warning signal, which is followed by escape or attack.

Fear and aggression. These two emotions are very close to each other. An unexpected noise, a threatening look, a new smell, an unknown animal or a strange person can cause uncertainty, fear or aggression. An animal stressed by any of these emotions can even become aggressive towards a loved companion, which is difficult for us to understand. However, this is normal and a part of their everyday life.

Attack. A vicious attack can follow threatening behaviour. This can frighten inexperienced pet owners. Sparks will fly! The rabbits jump in the air, kick with their hind legs, hit with their front legs and bite, which can leave the opponent with a loss of fur or even with wounds. As will be mentioned later in this book, it all looks much worse than it is. If the habitat is large enough and provides enough retreats, then there is no reason to panic.

Happiness. Rabbits can also express joy through their behaviour. With perky, hopping jumps and agile darting they show that they are thoroughly happy. Let us take this as a thank you for providing them with an appropriate habitat, caring for them and showing an understanding for their ways and behaviour.

> Rabbits show their gratitude for our efforts to look after them and respect their needs with perky behaviour, which is an expression of their happiness.

Setting up a group of rabbits

When setting up a successful group of rabbits, it is important that we consider the characters of the individual animals, their gender and their age. Race and size, however, are less important. Small animals are usually a little faster and cheekier, whilst the larger rabbits are slower and more placid.

Combinations

If only two rabbits are kept together, then it is best to choose a male and a female, because they accept each other more quickly. As far as keeping them in a group is concerned, it should be noted that castrated male rabbits are more peace-loving than male guinea pigs, and more placid than unspayed females. It should also be mentioned that young animals need other youngsters and an adult animal needs a more mature partner. Although a young animal might be accepted quickly, it would not, in the sometimes fierce fights for hierarchy, be physically strong enough, which could end in fatal injuries.

9 The unique social behaviour

When putting together a group of rabbits, breed is not important - the crucial factors are character and gender.

To create better dynamics when creating a group, we always suggest having three to four animals and, if possible, having them right from the start, as integrating a new rabbit creates a lot of stress. If a pair of rabbits have been living together over a longer period of time and are adjusted to each other, it is advisable to integrate two more animals. If just one rabbit is introduced, it may end up living a life as the odd man out, even though it might be accepted with time.

There are several combinations possible in a group:

- A castrated male and two to three females
- Two castrated males and two to four females
- Only castrated males in small groups

There are other possible combinations. The successful make-up of the group is more dependent on the character of the animals than on numbers and gender.

Only males. It may be surprising but it is true – several males can live very harmoniously in small groups, as long as they are, without exception, castrated and not too domineering. Adult uncastrated males will definitely attack each other.

Only females. A female group is not recommended, as females can often deal with each other in a bitchy and aggressive way. If, however, one castrated male is amongst them, this will have a very calming effect on the animals. The male arbitrates and does not react to attacks by the females.

> To avoid stress, it is advisable to make up a group of three to five rabbits from the very beginning.

There are no loners

■ *"Our Tappy is a loner. We have tried several times to give him one or the other companion, but he has not accepted any of them."*

The opinion that a rabbit which has lived alone for a long time will not integrate in a group, is wrong. For over twenty years we have put together hundreds of groups and we have learnt that there are no loners – just difficult animals and impatient owners. To adjust the rabbits to one another, a fair amount of knowledge and consideration is needed. It also requires much patience, intuition, steady nerves and the readiness to accept that there may be a very turbulent and long adjustment period.

> Even though rabbits are very social animals, the adjustment is often difficult and requires much preparation, knowledge and patience.

Dealing with adjustment

Neutral ground. The adjustment of strangers is easiest on neutral ground, where they can stay for a while with none of them having claimed its territory. Then, placing them in the run may still cause hierarchy fights, but they will be less severe.

Cleaning and re-designing the territory. There is another possibility. If a single rabbit is to receive a partner or a group is having animals added to it, we can remove them from their usual environment for a few days. The run is then cleared and all fittings cleaned carefully. A new habitat can then be created with the help of fresh materials from woods and gardens.

A well-constructed run makes the adjustment of new rabbits easier. They should always be able to recover from stress out of sight of the established animals.

Finally, everything is then covered with fresh bark bedding. It is important that the animals have many hideouts, pipes, corners and niches. Only then should all the animals, old and new, be put back together.

> Several hideouts and natural gnawing material simplify the integration of a new animal into an existing group.

Long adjustment period. It is important that we prepare ourselves for a demanding adjustment period – for us and the animals – which could take anything from three days to three weeks, and in extreme cases up to six months. During this time there can be severe fights for the hierarchy and the animals are exposed to more stress. It is difficult for us pet owners to deal with this. We must be prepared to accept this phase and not give up at the first problem. Occasionally, the first phase of putting the rabbits together is free from conflict and we assume that it must be love at first sight, but this impression can be deceiving. The animals will usually start their fights for supremacy a few days later. Once the rabbits have settled down, they will lead a reasonably peaceful life for many years.

> Unlike other animals, an adult rabbit should never have a young companion, as this can become dangerous and even end in death.

Groups of young animals. With very young rabbits, the adjustment period does not normally create a problem. For this reason, it is preferable to create the group whilst the animals are still young.

Fights for hierarchy during the adjustment period

When joining together a group of strangers, the adjustment period can take several weeks to months and the battle for supremacy can sometimes be quite harsh. During that time, fights are normal. We do not like what we see here - instead of peacefully sniffing and playing with each other, the animals perform mad chases with fights, and at times bite each other. Startled and frightened, a rabbit might retreat and avoid further contact with the attacker.

Pity or panic is inappropriate

Despite your love of animals, you must use reason and not pity. It is understandable that we feel sorry for the rabbits and would like to help, but we do them no favours if we pull them apart. Harsh fights during the adjustment period are normal and should not give us any reason to worry. We need to keep calm and clearheaded, otherwise there is a danger that our anxiety will transfer to the animals and make their hierarchy fights unnecessarily more difficult. It is more important to make sure that the fixtures of the run are good, so that the animal can retreat to recover out of sight of the other animals. Fresh branches and roots to gnaw on help to occupy the rabbits and therefore reduce their aggression.

Subconsciously, we might expect a reward for our efforts to help these animals and are disappointed that they do not appreciate this by living peacefully together. Gradually, however, we see that it is the same with rabbits as it is with people. You cannot live peacefully with everyone all the time.

It is vitally important to provide numerous caves, niches, dry places and elevated areas.

Not just 'trying', but rather persevering

If we start something with the attitude of, 'let's try it', we immediately include failure in our plans. Steely determination, not hesitation, promises success and we need strong nerves to endure. If we try something, and after a few days give up, we cause unnecessary stress to the rabbits, as a new attempt will be needed if we do not want to sentence the animal to a solitary life. An overnight separation for the animal to recover should be avoided, as the next day this fight for hierarchy will start all over again and this constant stress could be deadly. Measured by the long life of a rabbit, the adjustment period of a few hard weeks or months is relatively short and is worth enduring. The most important rules, therefore, are not to interfere and not to separate the animals, not even temporarily. Incidents will normally only happen if the animals are severely obese or do not have enough retreats. You will often see bites in the fur or the pulling out of bundles of hair. The animals can incur wounds and scratches, especially on their ears, because the skin is exposed and sensitive in this area. This usually looks worse than it is and rarely needs treatment.

> The recipe for success during the adjustment period is: be patient; do not lose your nerve; persevere; and, above all, do not separate the animals.

Observe eating habits

It is much more important to assess the general health and feeding behaviour of the rabbits than worry about wounds and scratches. Does it appear at feeding time? If a rabbit does not leave the hutch or does not dare come out of its hideout, we should put the food in front of it. There are cases when it is sensible to take a rigid animal out of its isolation and put it in the centre of the run. During the adjustment period, the animals require a great deal of energy and it is essential that they eat. At this time we are allowed to give them any food, even bread or gnawing sticks. The only important thing is that all the rabbits eat. If this is the case, we can assume that none of the animals are suffering excessively and that they are coping with the adjustment stress.

> During the adjustment period the rabbits need a lot of food for energy and their feeding behaviour must be observed very carefully.

After the fight comes the love

It can create havoc when strangers are getting to know each other and establishing the hierarchy. This does not mean that two animals do not suit each other. Quite the opposite, sometimes they attack each other dreadfully at the beginning and after two weeks, or sometimes months, they become inseparable. How lovely it is to see the two enemies licking and being together constantly. The worst bullies can turn into lambs after a few days. That is the point where you can be proud of yourself, as you have survived their adjustment period.

9 The unique social behaviour | 121

> Even though rabbits live in groups and keep close social contact, each animal requires its own territory, which it will defend. In a group with insufficient room, there will always be a certain restlessness because the various territories overlap.

After vicious fights during the adjustment period, great affection can often be seen amongst the rabbits.

It is possible that healthy animals will still occasionally fight, sometimes quite hard, but this is completely natural and should not worry you.

> Even in a well-functioning rabbit group, it is not always peaceful. Wild chases are part of their lively everyday habits.

When is intervention necessary?

Even in the best-selected group, an animal can become an outcast or behave like a rabbit Rambo. In such cases we will have to act to prevent long-lasting damage. Our intervention is necessary when a rabbit:

- seems to be suffering
- is hardly seen or not integrated in the group for a longer period
- keeps no social contact with other animals
- constantly has wounds from bites
- remains in the same corner for one or two days and does not eat

Such an animal must not be kept on its own out of pity. We do it no favours this way. It should be put with an animal of the same strength or weakness, or possibly a young animal.

Conditions for the successful grouping of rabbits

- Well-structured run of at least 6 square metres (for 2-3 animals)
- Many protected hideouts
- Enough natural gnawing material to keep them occupied
- Placement of all animals at the same time in a clean, well-structured run
- No 'female-only' groups
- Males must always be castrated (even brothers)
- Despite small injuries, no interference in their fights to establish hierarchy
- Keeping calm and giving the animals time to adjust
- Carefully observing their general health and eating habits

The gentle adjustment method

Even a rabbit which has been kept on its own for years can, with the help of so-called 'gentle adjustment', get used to a partner or a group. It is advisable to use this kind of adjustment for rabbits that have health problems, are obese or over-anxious. This method can also be used when an owner is not very patient.

A box with plenty of hay can give a rabbit the necessary feeling of security.

When using gentle adjustment, part of the run should be separated off and a crate with plenty of hay placed on its side. In this area, the new animal can get adjusted for a few days or weeks. After some time, this divider is removed. It is possible that the rabbits will still attack each other, but at least the new rabbit can retreat into a place it already knows. This way it can be integrated slowly and with less stress. In time, the food should be placed in the middle of the run, so that the rabbits can slowly get used to each other.

When two rabbits are separated

Circumstances can lead to a separation of two animals that have been friends for a long time and are very close. This is a very big issue for rabbits. Without their beloved partner, the world is not the same any more.

Temporary separation

To our way of thinking, it does not seem to matter if we separate rabbits for a few hours or days, but rabbits experience things differently. Their short-term memory causes them not to recognise even the closest partner after a short separation. We might call it 'out of sight, out of mind'. When the animals are put back together again, they have become strangers and fall back into their old ways of attacking each other. But even here there is an exception to the rule. Occasionally it does happen that the memory persists for a longer time and after a short separation there is a happy reunion.

However, as this is not the norm, we should try not to separate the animals, even for a few hours. They should also not be separated if they become sick, because by then the other animal will already have been infected anyway. A rabbit that is unwell or in pain needs its companions all the more. If it is suddenly on its own, its will to live can dwindle.

> Rabbits should, whenever possible, not be separated, not even temporarily.

Death of a rabbit

When a rabbit dies, the remaining rabbit desperately needs a new partner very quickly. A rabbit only 'grieves' because it is on its own. Grieving as we humans know it does not exist in rabbits. We have to provide a mature partner for an adult, as a young animal would be too playful and much weaker, which could become dangerous.

Humans and rabbits

Even an animal which lives together with animals of the same species will come to its owner if approached with patience and intuition. Such a relationship can become very rewarding, but it is important always to approach the animal carefully and slowly. Sudden movements can cause them to flee. If we crouch down to feed the rabbits by hand and calmly speak to them, they will get used to our body smell and the sound of our voice. Animals tamed this way will enjoy it if we gently touch and stroke them. From then on they seem to await our arrival with pleasure and curiosity.

10 Reproduction and birth control

Half of all rabbits are males, even in domesticated animals. In the wild, several males live with their females and offspring in family unions and their reproduction rate is enormous. But, as rabbits have many natural enemies, their numbers are constantly reduced. Besides that, they have a large habitat at their disposal where they can avoid each other. The conditions for our domesticated animals are quite different. They live in confined areas and without enemies. We therefore have to limit their reproduction in a different way, by neutering.

> In the era of animal protection and neutering, keeping rabbits individually should never be a method of birth control.

Neutering

By neutering we mean the surgical removal of the reproductive organs – ie testicles for males and ovaries for females. Usually, only the males are castrated. This is a routine operation in a veterinary practice and is conducted under full anaesthetia, which is painless for the animals. Castrated males are generally very peaceful and good-natured animals. As long as they are not unusually territorial, several males can live peacefully together.

■ *"I want to keep my animals naturally and not interfere with nature by castrating them. I just can't do it."*

To breed any animal taken into captivity is, in itself, a major interference in nature and forces us to take further steps, especially regarding birth control. The separation of females from males is the worst solution to the reproduction problem. It would follow that males would be kept alone as uncastrated animals because they would constantly fight with each other if kept together. If we want to adopt the natural family structure from the wild, then there is only one solution: castration. This is an unavoidable

10 Reproduction and birth control

Castrated male rabbits are mostly very peaceful animals and are often much more adaptable than females.

fact for the appropriate care of rabbits. In this age of animal protection, castration is the only choice to allow animals to be kept in groups.

> Domesticated rabbits can only be kept appropriately if their uncontrolled reproduction is prevented through neutering, which also helps to reduce aggression amongst males.

The castration of male rabbits

What is the effect of castration in males?

- It allows us to keep males and females together without them producing offspring.
- The fight for females ceases and the group becomes more peaceful.
- Castration makes it possible to put together a male group, as castrated males are mostly very peaceful animals. They are placid, well-balanced and often more trusting than females.
- With one or several males in the group, the activities of the rabbits are much livelier and more varied and this benefits the animals and us.
- Bitchiness, which is often apparent between females, is neutralised by the males. They keep the peace and are a calming influence on the group.

In the past, only female rabbits were sold or placed together, or a young male and a guinea pig. Today, responsible pet owners consider what happens to the surplus males and also whether the above-mentioned combinations are really species-appropriate. For a long time no-one spoke about this and many animals were simply 'disposed of'.

Over many years, when re-homing males, we have discovered that it is quite possible to keep several castrated males together in a peaceful social environment, so long as the basic conditions of species-appropriate care are fulfilled. This is not the case if several uncastrated males live together, because in this situation aggression and serious injuries will definitely take place.

Castration of a sexually mature male

It is important to differentiate between the castration of an animal which has reached sexual maturity and the so-called 'early castration' of sexually immature males. At the age of about 10 to 11 weeks, a rabbit becomes fertile (smaller breeds even earlier and larger types a little later). The whole reproductive system is fully functional at this point. After the operation, in which both testicles are removed, the animal will stay fertile for one to two weeks because some sperm is left in the sperm sac. In exceptional cases this time span can be longer. With the hormonal changes, the strong sexual odour decreases and very often also their frequent marking of territory. Older rabbits can still be castrated, as nowadays there are anaesthetics which reduce the danger of accidents to a minimum, even in older animals.

> You should consider birth control for your rabbits at an early stage. A sexually premature male can already be fertile at an age of 8 weeks.

Early castration

Early castration is carried out before the animal becomes fertile, at a weight of 600-900 grammes and an age of approximately 8-10 weeks. The reproductive system is not yet active at this point, as the testicles have not descended into the scrotum, so the operation places considerable demands on the veterinary surgeon.

Advantages of early castration

- Early-castrated rabbits are never fertile and therefore do not have to be separated from the group, not even temporarily.
- They recover much quicker from the anaesthetic.
- The strong sexual scent never occurs.

- When re-homing, harmonious small groups can be put together (eg a pair, or a male and two females).
- Long-term studies have shown that there are no negative results or side-effects, also regarding the growth of the animals.

> Many problems can be solved if male rabbits are castrated early.

Early castration means no separation from the group.

Spaying female rabbits

It is not yet widely known that female rabbits can also be neutered. They react in different ways when they are in heat. Some are very well-balanced, whilst others are plagued by their hormones and become very fussy and bitchy during that time. They are in heat every two weeks if the female is not mated. Sometimes they rebel and mount their companions or have false pregnancies. They prepare a nest, pull out their fur or collect all sorts of material to pad their nest. If this behaviour becomes a nuisance, or if it creates unrest in the group, neutering should be considered. The operation is more complicated, but an experienced vet can carry out this procedure without any problems. The advice to spay females is mainly aimed at those owners who keep their animals indoors where, due to restricted space and lack of activity, this kind of behaviour can become a problem. Besides that, the high incidence of uterus cancer is also a strong argument for spaying females.

Rabbit offspring

"We planned everything well and many friends promised they would take the young rabbits. Now they have all withdrawn their offers."

The wish to experience rabbits with their babies just once is understandable. Actually letting it happen often brings unsolvable problems rather than pleasure. For animal welfare reasons and because of the fact that many animals, even young ones, cannot be placed, we would not advise anyone to breed or allow even one litter. The number of rabbits being handed into animal shelters is on the increase and they often have to wait a very long time to be placed into a good home. The following information is directed at owners who have to deal with unplanned rabbit offspring.

Pregnancy. When a female has mated, the pregnancy is almost never noticeable until the end. An increase in the size of its stomach is certainly rarely discernable. The duration of a pregnancy is about 30 days and a novice will not realise until the last few days, when the female starts to build a nest, that she is going to give birth.

Nest. In an outside run, the mother digs a hole before she gives birth, which she covers until the young ones are allowed to leave the nest after two to three weeks. She then leaves it open over a longer period of time and the offspring come to the entrance, first at night and then, eventually, in daytime. As soon as someone comes near they all disappear immediately. In a hutch, the rabbit mother finds herself a dark place as a substitute for a cave, where she can give birth and then shield the babies. For this reason, if a pregnancy is suspected, a birth box or little 'house' should be provided in readiness.

Birth. We suggest that you do not make any changes in the habitat or the group structure and that the castrated male remains with the female (see page 135, Repeat mating). If the animals are kept appropriately, we do not have to fear that the father will kill the babies. This danger only exists if they are kept in a cage where the mother has no way of making a proper nest and where the animals do not have enough room. The birth is normally without any complications and goes unnoticed by us. Very often the covering of the nest and the shutting up of the cave are the only signs that the rabbit has given birth. The number of babies varies from three to twelve and increases with each litter.

Newborns. The babies are nestlings that are born naked and blind. The mother feeds them every 24 hours for a few minutes and only when she is not being watched. The animals should therefore remain in the dark and should be left alone. After ten days the rabbits open their eyes and become increasingly active.

Handling. If the young ones are born in a cage, we can now start with the so-called 'handling'. We should pick up the animals very gently, without taking them out of the nest, and get them used to being handled. Only a grown-up should do this, as the babies can suddenly jump from your hand, which could be dangerous for them. You could object to this

The babies are fed once a day for several minutes. At all times they should be kept in the dark where they can rest without being disturbed by us.

handling and argue that nature should take its course and the babies develop without human intervention. We would argue against this because tame animals give more pleasure and are easier to care for.

Young animals. Rabbits that have been born naturally in a burrow leave their nest after two weeks (at the earliest) and, at first, only appear at night. It is slightly more difficult to tame them. It requires time, a calm approach and good intuition. The rabbit father now cares lovingly for the youngsters too.

They will eat by themselves at four weeks but they do still need their parents. It is absolutely essential for their physical and psychological development to keep the young animals in their family environment for at least ten weeks.

10 Reproduction and birth control

Determination of gender. An experienced person can determine the gender immediately after the babies are born. For an inexperienced person it is a little more difficult and even experts can be wrong, which can have unexpected results. It is therefore an advantage if two experts determine the gender.

Repeat mating. If a rabbit father has not been castrated, or is castrated less than ten days before the birth of the babies, a repeat mating can take place on the day of the birth. To nurse and be pregnant again creates a double strain for the rabbit mother. After 28 days she would then have to get the young animals out of the nest to provide for the new birth, which can mean withdrawal problems for the first litter.

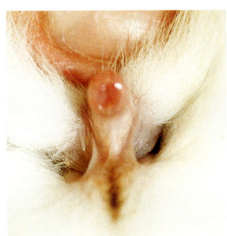

Above left: Male rabbit

Above right: Female rabbit

Left:
An experienced person can, through slight pressure in the stomach area, push the penis forward.

10 Reproduction and birth control

They also would still like some milk and the warmth of the nest. In such cases the babies can die after three to four weeks because they are stressed and can become infected, more often than not, by parasites in the gastrointestinal tract (coccidiosis). They leave behind an emaciated mother.

> Be careful: On the day of the birth the rabbit mother can mate again. The rabbit father should be castrated at least ten days before the birth, because he would like to – and should – be present on this important occasion.

Reproduction rate. "Breeding like rabbits". Never was an expression more apt! Rabbits in the wild are defenceless, so nature compensates for the large loss of life with high reproduction rates. For us pet owners, a litter of six animals can lead on to a family of fourteen, just two months after we have bought two sweet young rabbits. There is not enough room in the run and we have to give some away, but we do not have much time to do this, as sexual maturity for the first litter is already underway. Considering all these problems, we ask you to guard against such multiplication in the interest of the rabbits.

> Being responsible and acting in the interests of the animal should mean giving up the idea of having baby rabbits. Children are also capable of understanding the reasons for not letting rabbits give birth.

Sexual maturity

Sexual maturity means having the capability to reproduce. This happens before the animals are grown up. The beginning of sexual maturity is dependent on the breed and weight of a rabbit. The size of the litter also plays a big role. In smaller breeds, the sexual maturity happens earlier, normally at ten to twelve weeks. In larger breeds this can sometimes happen a little later, but at any rate long before they are grown up.

It is important to realise that young males can impregnate their mother and sisters very soon. This leads to interbreeding and all the resulting complications.

Breeding maturity

A female rabbit is only mature and strong enough for breeding when her physical development allows her to get pregnant and give birth without any problems. The breeding maturity in females begins at around six to eight months, when the animals are almost grown up. Females should never be mated before then, because although they are becoming sexually mature, they are still youngsters. If we keep two young rabbits for the purpose of breeding at a later date, then they have to be separated at a young age to avoid the risk of reproduction. This, however, is not appropriate caring. A female should not be mated too early or too late. If she is older than two years, complications can occur at the birth, or the babies could be stillborn or handicapped in some way.

> **The initial excitement of having baby rabbits just once very often turns into a nightmare, due to unforeseen and insurmountable problems. This should be considered very carefully before deciding to go ahead with it.**

11 Nutrition and digestion

Correct and balanced nutrition forms the basis for a healthy rabbit life. Modern feeding with vitamin drops and gnawing sticks, which have become a common method over the last few years, is only convenience food that makes life very easy for the pet owner. You buy a bag of ready-mixed food once a month and put a cupful in their dish. But our rabbits deserve something better – varied and properly balanced meals. To find out more, we should look at how wild rabbits eat.

Herbivores

Rabbits living in the wild eat roots, bark, herbs, twigs and fresh plants. They spend most of the day looking for food and are almost constantly eating. They swallow a lot of raw fibre with the plants, which shows how important dry grass (hay) is for our domesticated rabbits.

> **Herbivores must have the opportunity to eat continuously. Plenty of fresh hay is necessary to stimulate digestion.**

Like all herbivores, rabbits can digest their food only with the help of special bacteria, which is able to break up cellulose. Every food component needs specific bacteria and this creates a complicated and precarious balance. The intestinal flora is always active, even when the animals are fed incorrectly, are very hungry or the intestine is idle. Indigestion problems can become apparent very quickly, as certain bacteria increase drastically (enterotoxaemia), and because of the creation of gas, the rabbit can develop painful and dangerous bloating (tympany).

The digestive system of rabbits

Ruminant animals like cows, sheep and goats have, unlike rabbits, a highly elaborate stomach system which allows them to keep their digestion active without having to eat (ruminal digestion). After a feed in the fields, the animals lie down, regurgitate the food bit by bit and chew it again. During this process they get rid of fermenting gases by burping. The rumen is, in relation to their body, very large and equipped with strong muscles, because they have to knead the food through to make it accessible to pre-digesting bacteria and transport it into the intestine.

Large intestine digestion

As with horses and guinea pigs, the stomach of rabbits only serves as a reception container and is relatively small. The contents of the stomach are not moved actively by the weak muscle wall, but mechanically by the new amount of food consumed. To prevent the digestion coming to a standstill, it is important to keep on eating. The bacterial breakdown of the cellulose takes place in the large intestine. Rabbits are prone to bloating (tympany) because it is difficult to get rid of fermenting gasses out of the large intestine.

Because of their weak-muscled stomachs, rabbits are unable to vomit. The capacity of the stomach is very small, approximately 40ml, and must always be full up. Because of this small stomach volume, rabbits can only eat a little at a time and therefore have to eat continuously. Animals in the wild visit their feeding places up to 80 times a day, but if they eat too much food at one time (eg after a hunger phase or when eating bloating foods), it can overload the stomach or, because of the thin stomach wall, can even cause a tear.

> The digestive system of herbivores must always be in motion. Spending a few days without food, which is not necessarily dangerous for carnivores, must not happen to herbivores.

Caecotrophs (special droppings)

A peculiarity in rabbits is the eating of caecotrophs, which are rich in vitamin B. Through this, the nutrition in the food can be absorbed a second time round and therefore be used more efficiently. The caecotrophs are mainly passed at night and immediately eaten again. If some are left over, they lie in the form of light grape-like shapes in the run and are not to be confused with diarrhoea.

Eating all day long

Rabbits are constant eaters. As their diet consists of plants, they can suffer very quickly from digestion problems if fed improperly. We have to ensure that we feed them appropriate food that they can eat all day long. However, this does not mean that we should give them all their food, like hay, greenery and grain, in the morning. We should, in fact, feed our rabbits three times a day and follow a certain sequence. We do not put the soup, main course and dessert on the table at the same time. A rabbit will behave like a child: it will start with the dessert, try a little of the main course and then have no more room for the soup.

The selection of food is of great importance. As rabbits eat constantly, they depend on a balanced diet so they do not become obese. The basic food is hay and water and these should be given to them first thing in the morning. They are essential for survival and cannot be replaced with anything else.

> Rabbits have to be fed at least three times a day.

11 Nutrition and digestion

The daily feeding of hay is the secret of healthy nutrition.

Hay is the most important thing

■ *"My rabbits always have more than enough hay in the rack, I refill it at least every second day."*

Even when our rabbits still have hay in the rack in the morning, we must always replace it with fresh hay; not only in the rack but heaped in various places in the run and also spread as bedding in the hutch and other places of rest. The hay from yesterday is stale and does not entice the rabbits to eat it. This is a very important point, if not the most important of all, for a healthy, problem-free digestion.

Hay is rich in raw fibre and relatively tough. The animals eat slowly and chew constantly so that a lot of saliva is produced. The saliva optimises the conditions for intestinal bacteria and stimulates the digestion.

For this reason the rabbits should be offered sufficient hay in the morning. This has been practised in the feeding of herbivores for hundreds of years on farms.

> **The correct sequence when feeding is of great importance. The rabbits' day has to begin with lots of hay.**

This then becomes a real ritual. The animals come to the feeding area, even if they are not particularly hungry, which gives us a good opportunity to talk to them. Changes in behaviour can best be noticed when the rabbits are feeding.

Hay is not always hay

We should pay careful attention to the quality of the hay. Good hay is green, not yellow or brown, smells aromatic and is well ventilated, dry and loose in the rack. It must not be dusty, mouldy or musty, as this could cause serious digestive problems. We must not economise when buying hay. If there is sufficient room to store it, it is best bought in large quantities directly from a farmer. In the interest of his own animals, he produces good quality hay.

Water

■ *"Our animals made the water dirty and tipped their dish but never drank any of it, so we are not putting water in a dish anymore."*

Rabbits need a lot of water (even in winter), on average 2dl (6.5 oz.) daily. This is a fair amount and is equivalent to half a litre (a pint) for three animals. Although some of the required liquid can be provided by green food, we must always supply plenty of fresh water.

They should never feel thirsty and find that there is no water. Lack of liquids can lead to kidney troubles in animals as well as humans.

Terracotta dish

Water is best served in a heavy terracotta dish. To avoid immediate soiling, we suggest it is put on an elevated place (eg on a brick). This way the animals do not walk in it or knock it over.

> Rabbits always have to be supplied with fresh water in a wide, open dish.

Water bottle

The ubiquitous water bottles should never be used with rabbits. As the bottles only allow the rabbits to drink drop by drop, the animals have trouble to quench their thirst. If they have to stretch to reach the bottle, the unnatural position makes swallowing difficult. We should follow nature where water and drinking methods are concerned.

Drinking bottles are also difficult to keep clean. The temptation to quickly refill the bottle without cleaning it is always there. Besides that, it is almost impossible to clean the bottle, as the tube and nipple are very small. On warm days algae forms very quickly, which is not easy to see but creates a slimy layer on the inside of the bottle. The popularity of this kind of bottle stems from the time of small cages and is anchored deeply in the psyche of pet owners. Every rabbit will easily adjust if faced with an open dish of water. At times, when watching them with their dish of water, we get the impression that they are compensating for a chronic lack of liquid in the past.

Feeding plan

If possible, we should feed our rabbits three times a day. The day begins, as mentioned earlier, with water and a load of fresh, good quality hay, which is spread in all dry places in large quantities so that our rabbits can find fresh bits all through the day and night. At noon, a few hours after spreading the hay, we should give them the greenery. The last meal is the rabbit mix in the evening. This feeding sequence has proved itself. Given in this order, all the various foods are good for them and do not cause them any indigestion.

Daily Feeding

- morning - fresh hay and water
- midday - greenery
- evening – grain (rabbit mix)

If you give the animals their favourite food (greenery) before or together with the hay, they will attack this first and not eat their hay, which can lead to acute tympany. Besides that, it can cause stomach and intestinal problems which can develop slowly over months or years.

Frequent feeding errors

- hay not fed fresh daily
- not enough hay (ie only in the rack)
- hay and greenery together
- greenery first thing in the morning (extremely dangerous)

Greenery

Contrary to advice in various books, greenery is very appropriate food for rabbits and provides them with the necessary vitamins. Providing successful and digestible greenery is a matter of habit, as well as the amount and the sequence of the feeding. It is best done at lunchtime, a few hours after providing hay. At this time the digestive system is already working and the animals do not suffer from bloating. If, at any time, this sequence cannot be followed, the gap between feeding can be shortened. It is, however, important to feed the greenery two to three hours after feeding hay. Kitchen waste is not suitable for rabbits. The remaining food should be removed before the next greenery is fed.

> Rabbits love greenery. It must, however, be given to them a few hours after the fresh hay has been fed, to avoid bloating.

A few hours after feeding fresh hay, the greenery is a healthy and popular supplement.

Daily rations

We suggest the following daily feed per rabbit:

- A carrot or half a fennel
- Some apple pieces
- In summer – dandelion, grass and field herbs
- In winter – wild lettuce, curly kale, savoy cabbage or other salads.

Apple regulates the digestion and prevents intestinal problems. Curly kale does not cause bloating if given at the right time - quite the opposite, as it has medicinal properties that have been used successfully for hundreds of years. With its high vitamin C content, curly kale prevents illnesses. The following vegetables and fruits can also be offered to the rabbits; pears, broccoli, forage beet, celeriac, spinach, endive, various herbs (eg sage).

Feeding changes

When adding a new feeding component, there must not be an abrupt change, and extra hay must be given in the morning. A new food should always be introduced slowly and in small amounts so that the digestive system can adjust. This is especially the case in spring with fresh grass, which is juicy and rich in protein and can lead to bloating. What this means is starting with small rations and increasing them over several days.

Poisonous plants

Animals fed with varied food and which also always have plenty of gnawing material will not rush over to eat poisonous plants like thuja and yew. Field herbs do not have to be sorted but they should not be freshly fertilised or collected near the edge of a road. No-one would deliberately give their animals poisonous herbs.

Daily monitoring

We suggest daily monitoring during the feeding of greenery or grain. This should always be done by the same adult, who knows what he/she is doing. We check if all the animals come to feed and how they eat. If any animal is missing, we look for it and follow this up after a few hours.

The daily monitoring must be done by a responsible and knowledgeable adult.

If a rabbit really is not eating, it should be seen by a vet on the same day. Further signs to observe in the animals can be found in the following chapter, Health is no coincidence.

> Lack of appetite is always an alarm signal, which should be taken seriously. Unlike dogs and cats, rabbits cannot stop eating for even a day, as their digestion must never rest.

Rabbit mix

Grain is an energy and strength food that has to be fed carefully, as rabbits tend to get obese. We cannot advise on amounts because there are too many factors like type, size, exercise, age and general health that influence how the food is absorbed. Quality food consists of a good mixture of various grains with all the necessary vitamins and minerals. (We recommend quality rabbit food from E. Schweizer Samen AG, CH - Thun.)

With low-energy activity in summer, a light feed without maize, sunflower seeds, peanuts and the like should be offered, and there should be no bread given. This changes when there is high-energy activity.

The following need high-energy food:

- Rabbits kept outdoors in winter
- Growing animals
- Suckling and pregnant females
- Convalescent and underweight animals
- Stressed animals in the adjustment phase

As each animal puts on a different amount of fat, your intuition and common sense should help with feeding the animals accordingly.

Gnawing material

Gnawing material such as branches, twigs, bark and roots are enormously important to keep the rabbits occupied and to wear down their incisor teeth. Even though dwarf rabbits and rabbits are not classed as rodents, they have a very strong gnawing urge. During this activity they wear down their continuously growing teeth.

If offered on a regular basis, branches of red pine, fruit tree, beech and hazel are all suitable gnawing materials which serve as non-fatty food as well as hideouts and shade providers, helping to improve the animals' quality of life. Illness-causing bacteria are not brought into the run through the branches. The constantly replaced natural materials are stimulating and promote the vitality of the rabbits.

Red pine branches, beech and hazel bush twigs should always be present.

Bread

Bread is only good as gnawing material in exceptional cases. It allows the rabbit to nibble but is rich in calories. Of course this is different with sick and underweight animals, which have to be nurtured. Well-dried - but not mouldy - bread can help these animals to get back on their feet.

Winter feeding

In the cold winter months, the food for the rabbits should be rich in calories, as they need considerably more energy when living outdoors.

This means:
- Lots of fresh hay
- More energy food
- In addition, some hard bread

When the water freezes because the temperature is too low, it should be replaced with lukewarm water three times a day. The need for liquid is the same in winter as the rest of the year. Greenery is best served in their hutch so it does not freeze so quickly.

Extra food for ill animals

If a rabbit is not eating, it needs immediate veterinary attention. Under no circumstances must we wait any longer than the end of that day, as is possible with dogs and cats.

The digestion process in rabbits must never stop, so it is possible that extra feeding might be necessary. After dental treatment, an operation or illness, it is possible that the rabbits need our help to reactivate their digestive system. The best treatment is premium recovery food for herbivores and lactic-acid-producing bacteria (which are available from the vet) and to temporarily feed them with Darvida crackers, herbs and other tidbits plus vitamin drops.

Rearing orphaned animals

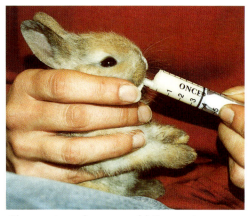

The rearing of young rabbits requires much patience and tranquillity.

If the young rabbits received some of their mother's milk before they were separated, bringing them up with a bottle can be successful. The rabbit has to be fed with a pipette, syringe or a special small baby bottle twice a day, preferably with kitten milk. Care has to be taken that no liquid gets into the windpipe, so the head must not be tipped back too much. The animals are woken up and fed until they refuse to drink any more. When finished, their little stomachs have to be carefully massaged towards the anus to activate the digestion. From the third week onwards we offer tender food like small pieces of apple, carrots and soft hay on a flat dish.

12 Health is no coincidence

The health of our rabbits depends predominantly on their habitat. The advent of illness is mostly the result of inappropriate keeping and feeding and not just fate. Stress and lack of hygiene can also make them prone to illness. The best provision for their good health is a healthy and balanced diet, appropriate keeping, and caring for their habitat on a regular basis. In such beneficial conditions, together with certain preventive measures, rabbits rarely become ill.

Cleanliness

When our rabbits are not kept in a clean environment, their health suffers, especially youngsters'. We should therefore muck out their hutches and runs regularly (once or twice weekly, depending on the number of animals) and remove their droppings on a daily basis. In hot weather, good hygiene is even more important, as parasites can be transferred through dirty food and soiled dishes. It is therefore obvious that we should offer our animals only clean food (not rotten or mouldy) and that we remove leftover food after 24 hours.

Observation

■ *"I have observed my animals really closely but I have not been able to pick them up. Now Flopsy is full of maggots," cries Severine. "How could this happen?"*

To notice signs of illness early, and to take the proper action, we have to observe our rabbits carefully on a daily basis. Additional weekly and monthly checks are also necessary, which should always be undertaken by a responsible and knowledgeable adult.

Children are not really in a position to notice small changes in the animals' behaviour and interpret them correctly. We recommend regular checks so that our rabbits do not end up in a life-threatening situation, due to a long illness which has not been noticed.

We should take time to observe our animals daily.

Daily checks

In daily contact with our animals, we should realise when an animal has tearful or misty eyes or a dripping nose, when the ears are not standing up or when it shows other changes in behaviour. Such changes can be visible in various forms and could include the rabbit doing the following:
- Sitting in a completely different place than normal
- Being lethargic and lying around all day
- Not appearing at feeding time
- Eating slower and more hesitantly than usual
- Appearing indifferent

Every change in behaviour is something which should be taken seriously. This requires intensive observation. If the rabbit is eating normally, a visit to the vet can be postponed. Be careful, though, because eye problems need immediate attention. As herbivores are not allowed to go a day without eating, immediate attention must be given if a lack of appetite appears. The intestine of a rabbit must not rest. For this reason it is important to make sure that all rabbits appear when feeding. If one is missing, we have to check a few hours later to see if it is eating. If not, then a visit to the vet is unavoidable.

> Every change in behaviour in a rabbit can be a sign of illness and must be taken seriously.

Weekly checks

- **Anal region**
  Is it clean and not sticky? Sticky fur must be cut away.
- **Chin and corners of mouth**
  Are they dry? Clammy corners of the mouth can be a sign of dental problems.

Monthly checks

- **Weight control**
  Has the rabbit put on or lost weight?
- **Fur control**
  Are crusts or loss of hair apparent?
- **Claws**
  Are they too long?
- **Teeth**
  Are they in good condition?

Carrying around

To check the animals over, we sometimes have to lift them. Rabbits can fight this by thumping fiercely with their legs. If we hold them too loosely they fidget, scratch and can free themselves. If we hold them too tightly they can easily break bones. Like the female rabbits carrying their young ones, we should pick them up by the fur of their neck and support them under the hind legs with the other hand. We then press the animal's legs towards us so that they cannot scratch. As rabbits do not like to be picked up, we should stroke them a lot and only carry them when it is absolutely necessary. Never lift them up by their ears. Rabbits have a very delicate body structure and should therefore only be carried by adults.

Checking the anus

The anal region should be clean and dry. Dirty and sticky parts of the fur should be carefully removed, which is best done with curved scissors. If it cannot all be removed, we can soak it with camomile tea. We put the rabbit in a bowl with camomile tea and soak the crusts for 10 minutes until they can be pulled off. The animal is then dried with a towel. In summer it is especially important to check the anus of older or problem animals, as the most dangerous parasites for rabbits are the numerous larvae of various flies. The droppings can stick to the fur and build a crust after a while, so that the skin below cannot breathe anymore and is susceptible to eczema.

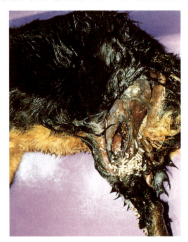

Problem animals should be checked daily in summer to avoid such an infestation of maggots.

In hot summer temperatures, flies lay their eggs on these damp areas and within a short time the larvae hatch and dig into the skin tissue around the rabbit's anus. After a few hours the maggots start eating the tissue. Unfortunately this problem appears very often and should be taken extremely seriously. To be eaten alive by maggots is a cruel death. Therefore it is advisable to check older, lazy or fat animals and those who suffer from diarrhoea on a regular basis - daily if necessary. Please note that fly larvae are often mistaken for worms.

Diarrhoea

Diarrhoea is a very serious alarm signal and can have various causes:
- Feeding error: lack of raw fibre (not enough, given at the wrong time, or not providing fresh hay daily) can lead to an enterotoxaemia, which stops normal fermentation in the digestive tract and causes bloating or diarrhoea.
- Gastro-intestinal parasites (Coccidia) or infectious disease (bacteria, viruses); worm infestation is rather rare.
- Dental problems: overlong incisors or cheek teeth prevent the continual, sufficient intake of high-fibre food and enough chewing of the food, which can lead to digestive problems.
- Stress.
- Rotten food.

Diarrhoea – Action to be taken

- Immediately provide plenty of fresh, good quality hay on a daily basis.
- Offer less juicy food, but more apple.
- Check its weight.
- Observe the animal well: if it does not eat enough, take it to the vet.

Dental check

Damp corners of the mouth or chin can point to a wrong position of the teeth. We should immediately check the weight of the rabbit and compare it with the previous registered weight. Has the animal lost weight? If it has not lost weight, we have to observe its eating behaviour carefully. If it is considerably lighter than at the last weighing time, we should visit the vet right away.

Rabbits have 28 teeth: In the upper jaw two incisors and two tiny peg teeth behind them, then six cheek teeth on each side. The lower jaw has two incisors and five cheek teeth on each side.

Rabbits' teeth grow all their lives at approximately 1-2mm per week, just like our fingernails. Due to the constant friction when eating, they wear each other down and this is the reason why we have to provide the animals with a variety of natural gnawing material in the form of branches, as well as plenty of hay, so they can keep on eating and chewing without putting on weight.

Healthy teeth are horizontally worn down and fit each other.

With badly worn-down teeth, the lower ones can grow forward between the lips.

...or the upper teeth grow against the tongue. An incorrect position before and...

...after the correction by the vet.

> **As a preventive measure to keep their teeth healthy, plenty of natural gnawing material in the form of new branches and twigs etc must be offered.**

The incisor teeth must meet vertically and get worn down horizontally. If the gnawing teeth are not worn down they bend like horns inwards and hinder the animal from eating, or they stick up between the lips. If in pain at the roots or in the jaw area, the rabbits chew on one side only, which causes one-sided wearing down of their gnawing teeth at an angle. It is also possible that cheek teeth can be worn down crookedly, which cannot be seen from the outside. If these do not wear down enough, the tips grow towards the tongue, injuring it and also the mucous membrane. This causes rabbits terrible pain and prevents them from eating – they can die of hunger sitting in front of a full dish. It is not always easy to notice this, as the animal, hungry as it is, will always be the first at feeding time and desperately try to eat. Only those who take the trouble to watch the eating habits of their animals carefully will see the early signs of a tooth problem.

Saliva-clustered fur around the chin can be a sign of this. Children are not really able to pin-point this and even adults can find it difficult.

Dental problems occur mainly in over-bred and smaller races. If we recognise a dental problem early enough, the vet can usually help. However, if you do not seek veterinary advice early enough, the rabbit will probably be weakened and its tongue injured. The healing process will be slower and oftentimes the animal will not survive.

Weight

After about eight months, a rabbit is grown and now its weight should be checked every month to make sure we notice if it loses or gains too much. Weight is dependent on size and build and the decisive point is not to keep to a weight norm but to the relative weight development of each rabbit. In other words, if a rabbit loses 10% of its bodyweight between two weight checks, then we have to observe the animal carefully and weigh it every second or third day. If it loses more than 10% we need help from a vet. A newborn rabbit weighs between 50-100g and an adult up to eight kilos, depending on the breed.

> Through regular recording of their weight, illnesses can be spotted earlier.

Fur care

Rabbits spend a lot to time caring for their fur and generally we do not have to do much in that area except check it once in a while. The fur should be shiny and have no bare spots.

This is different with long-haired rabbits, whose fur needs intensive care. Combing them on a daily basis, however, causes them stress, so we suggest that knots are cut out of their fur at least once a week. This prevents the fur becoming too matted and the necessity of having to shave the animal under an anaesthetic. Occasionally it may be necessary to brush short-haired rabbits when they moult.

Claws

Rabbits have five claws on the front paws and four on the back ones. If they can behave as they would in the wild, their claws will wear down by digging, hopping and darting. Rabbits kept indoors, however, mainly move on soft ground and their claws have to be cut from time to time, making sure not to damage the nail bed. It is best to do this under the supervision of an expert the first time around.

We should also check animals that live outdoors once a month. Older and lazy animals often do not wear down their claws properly. Claws that are too long hinder the animal's movement or force their toes into an unnatural position.

Claws that are too long hinder the animal's movement.

Bathing

Rabbits hate bathing and this procedure should therefore only be used if they are infested by mites or have a sticky area around their anus. Only the affected areas should be bathed. For this purpose we half-fill a basin with lukewarm water and put the animal in it. With calm, precise movements, the affected areas are then washed. It can be helpful and calming for the animal if a helper covers their eyes with their hand or a cloth.

Fungal skin disease

Round or oval spots on the skin are a typical sign of a fungal infection. If we notice these we should go and see a vet. The rabbits must be treated and washed with a fungal medication. These baths should be continued for six to eight weeks, as the infection can be very persistent. When animals are kept outdoors, a fungal infection can occur following a mosquito bite, which they will scratch until it bleeds. By scratching, the infection can be spread to other parts of the body. The changes under the skin can be much more advanced than is visible from outside. The affected areas must be treated liberally and intensively. Because the body gets rid of these changes from under the skin during the healing process, the spots can grow larger. This does not mean that the medication is not working, but is rather a sign of healing.

Parasites

Here we would only like to mention the parasites which are most common in rabbits. On the skin these are mites and in the intestine these are coccidia. Worm infestation is rare and if there is a suspicion that an animal is infested with something, it is most likely to be fly larvae, which are visible at the rabbit's rear-end. If you are not sure, take a sample to the vet's for further investigation.

Mites (Skin parasites)

If we suddenly notice dandruff-like areas on the skin, extensive fur loss, or if the animals scratch themselves intensively, they could be infected by mites. At this stage an injection will help.

Mites often appear in stress situations, when the immune system is weakened. The reasons for this may be adjusting problems, illness, loss of its order in the hierarchy or overcrowding in the run. It is up to us to find the cause and eliminate it. Natural materials from woods and gardens are not the cause of mite infestation, quite the opposite, they help prevent it. Occupied and interested animals are more resistant than bored ones.

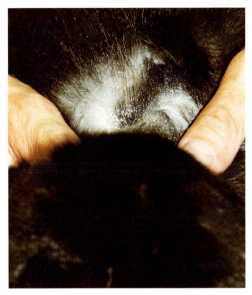

A rabbit infested with mites should be treated by a vet.

Coccidia (parasites in the gastro-intestinal tract)

Those who have dealt with rabbits for some time know that coccidiosis is a problem which needs to be taken seriously. The germs of this illness are one-celled parasites which exist in almost every rabbit's intestine. They are excreted in the droppings and can be easily transferred to other animals. Through contact with and the eating of the droppings, the animals can continually get infected in a vicious cycle.

Coccidia are diagnosed with the help of a microscope, but the number of eggs present does not indicate the stage of the illness, only how serious this excretion is. The animal can be infected with this illness even if there is no evidence of eggs in the droppings. If the coccidia increase, they can damage the liver, gallbladder and mucous membrane of the intestine. If the illness carries on, the blood vessels can be injured. Oozing blood will eventually make the animal anaemic and tired. If stronger bleeding occurs, this can result in hemorrhagic diarrhoea.

Stress situations can cause the increase of coccidia, which multiply drastically within a short time. We cannot, however, always avoid stress situations with our rabbits.

> Cleanliness in the run and especially in the feeding area can limit the danger of intestinal parasites.

Eating droppings

Do not be alarmed when your rabbits eat their droppings. The eating of caecotrophs is a nutritional physiological process that is necessary. This way the pre-digested food mash, which is rich in vitamins, is put through the digestive system in a kind of recycling. The caecotroph is normally eaten straight from the anus. It is soft and grape-like and must not be mistaken for diarrhoea. It is very different from the ordinary dry droppings.

Stress situations

Rabbits are very stress-sensitive animals. Various situations can be a strain on their immune system and make them prone to a variety of illnesses. We should therefore avoid, if possible, the following stress factors:

- unnecessary catching and picking up
- strange, loud children in the run
- a dog which chases them from outside the run
- loud, unknown noises

Certain situations cannot be avoided, but during the following situations we need to observe the rabbits carefully:

- re-homing
- adjusting into a new group
- descending in the hierarchy of the group
- mother rabbits: birth, suckling of the young animals (4-6 weeks)
- young animals: weaning

Stomach overload and tympany

These words should echo in the pet owner's head as the worst possible scenario. If we understand what they mean and what the causes are, the dangers can easily be eliminated.

Stomach overload

After a period of hunger, the rabbits will rush to their food. If we give them hay, which is rich in raw fibre, they eat slowly and have to chew. With that, a lot of saliva is produced and the digestion begins slowly. If, however, you give them food that they can gobble down, they will overeat. The overloaded stomach cannot be emptied due to the weak muscles. Generally the stomach then hardens and becomes larger.

Tympany

This is what we call bloating, which occurs due to incorrect fermentation in the large intestine during digestion and leads to a bloated abdomen. The affected rabbits have stomach-ache and lay around apathetically. Sometimes the bloated abdomen pushes onto the diaphragm, which can lead to respiratory distress. Incorrect fermentation is caused when:

- the animals are not used to greenery
- they eat greenery on an empty stomach
- greenery stays in the stomach after eating too much of it.

Such bloating in connection with stomach overloading can cause a tear in the stomach wall. Our rabbits must therefore not eat too much greenery in one go. If they spend the night in a hutch or in a small pen without grass, we should always offer them plenty of good quality hay before we let them out into the run. This way they can satisfy their hunger and the saliva produced during chewing activates the digestion. Greenery and grain are then eaten slower and digested better. The animals may otherwise rush to eat the grass, which can lead to a stomach overload with subsequent tympany.

If we are to avoid this problem of stomach overload we need to follow the feeding rules for herbivores:

- first hay, then greenery
- never let the rabbits go hungry.

> Greenery on an empty stomach is dangerous for rabbits. Hay, however, activates the digestion slowly and prevents stomach overload and poor fermentation.

Rabbits that have constant access to a grassy area will not over-eat. If they have the opportunity to eat as much as and when they like, they will only eat as much as is good for them. Therefore the stomach overload risk is almost eliminated. Fermentation problems do not exist,

12 Health is no coincidence

If we provide the rabbits with a lot of hay first thing in the morning, we prevent many problems.

because the animals are used to the steady eating of greenery and their digestion has adjusted to this.

Heatstroke

Rabbits are very sensitive to heat. They should never be locked in a small area such as a hutch. Cloths, awnings or small hutches can become death traps. Overweight animals and mohair rabbits are especially endangered. Fresh water and naturally-provided shade, like branches draped over roots, are extremely important. Should a rabbit lay as if dead on a hot day, do not panic and run to the vet, because the immediate transport of the animal under shock would probably finish it off. The animal should first be wrapped in a wet cloth and put in a cool, quiet place. The visit to the vet can be made later, if necessary.

Vaccinations

The idea of a vaccination is to give the animal protection against diseases which are difficult to treat. There are several vaccines available, the most important ones being against myxomatosis, pasteurellosis and viral haemorrhagic disease (VHD). There is always a debate as to whether to vaccinate or not. Most pet owners are familiar with the need to vaccinate cats and dogs, but not so where rabbits are concerned. The VHD vaccination is considered by many pet owners and experts as unnecessary. That attitude is surprising, considering that this was one of the most reported notifiable epidemics in Switzerland a few years ago. In the interest of rabbits, we hope that this disease will soon be extinct. It is important to plan the vaccinations according to the individual situation and condition of the animals, as well as the country they live in. Your vet can advise you when you go for the annual health check.

Illness

To understand illness in rabbits, which is a complex subject, requires expert knowledge. As the explanations of the multitude of symptoms and the pictures of illness would expand this book beyond measure, we have left this topic out.

For successful health precautions, the pet owner must be willing to observe his rabbit and be able to notice if it is unwell at an early stage, analyse it and visit a veterinary practice while there is still time to help.

Do not separate the sick rabbit from its companions

■ *"We took our Mopsy out of its group for only three days and now they are attacking each other again. How can this be possible?"*

As with humans, the psyche of an animal is affected during an illness. We should therefore not isolate an ill or injured animal, but leave it within its group and care for it there. The infection period is mostly before the outbreak of the illness, at a time before we know that the animal is sick.

If a rabbit is unwell, we have to take extra care with hygiene and feed all animals with a balanced diet which is rich in vitamins. If we separate the animals, even for a short while, we have to expect fights when rejoining them, as a new hierarchy has been established in the meantime. This would mean a new, stressful adjustment time for the convalescing animal. If it is still weak from the illness, it could have a relapse or, in the case of healing bones, a new fracture.

Even a sick animal needs contact with its companions.

Photo: E. Hunziker

Animals living in a harmonious group should hardly ever be separated from each other, not even temporarily. If a weak rabbit is set upon, bullied or threatened, we can separate a small area in the same run with wire mesh to allow the animal some peace. A sick rabbit which remains amongst its group has more will to live and recovers quicker than one that has been taken out of its usual environment.

> A sick rabbit has more will to live if it remains with its companions.

Visits to the vet

A yearly visit to a veterinary practice must be planned. At the same time as the vaccination, the animal should have a dental and general check-up. The rabbit is best transported in a cat basket or box that is not lined with straw or hay but with a bright cloth, which allows the expert to see the condition of urine and droppings. Too much room or light will make the animal insecure and anxious. Straw and hay are not suitable during transport, as they could injure the rabbit's eyes.

13 Keeping rabbits and guinea pigs together

If the conditions for keeping rabbits appropriately are fulfilled and the habitat is big enough, rabbits and guinea pigs can generally live peacefully with each other. Unfortunately this fact is very often used as a reason to keep one of each species only. The decision to combine one rabbit and one guinea pig is based on a series of misconceptions and prejudices that need to be corrected.

To each his own sleeping area.

Photo: S. Herrmann

13 Keeping rabbits and guinea pigs together

One rabbit and one guinea pig – the reasons behind a bad decision

Reasons, wrong assumptions	Correction
Because they understand each other.	It is only an assumed good relationship. The animals make the best of a bad situation because they are lonely.
To avoid castration.	In captivity all males should be castrated anyway (smell, dominance, biting, escaping).
Because conventional cages seem too small for two rabbits but large enough for a rabbit and a guinea pig.	Conventional cages are also too small for a single rabbit, let alone two. The suppression of the enormous urge for movement often leads to behavioural problems.
To avoid the adjustment period of two animals of the same species.	The simpler way is not the better way and is most certainly not species-appropriate.
To clear your conscience. This way you can avoid keeping a rabbit on its own.	It is still being kept on its own. Neither human nor other species contact can replace the essential social contact with the same species.
Because this has been advised and practised for years.	Not everything that has 'always been done this way' is really good.

Differences in the social behaviour of rabbits and guinea pigs

Rabbits and guinea pigs are both animals which live in groups; but other than that they are very different.

Rabbits	Guinea Pigs
Love cuddling and licking each other.	Keep their distance but will move along in each other's tracks.
Like to stay on elevated areas.	Will always look for places where they feel protected.
Dig and live in burrows.	Prefer covered hideouts.
Are mainly active at night.	Are active in the daytime and sleep in the hutch at night.
Express their love of life by darting and hopping.	Are jumpy, run from hideout to hideout and are always on the lookout for protection.
Mostly sleep on their own.	Mostly sleep close to each other.

This insight into the different social behaviour of the two animals makes it clear that each rabbit and each guinea pig needs at least one companion of the same species. Otherwise, although they are not alone, they still feel lonely.

Unfortunately, keeping two individual animals together is still practised and even recommended. It is debatable whether the reason for this is commercial, ignorance, carelessness or simply because of insufficient experience. Of course the adjustment of a rabbit and guinea pig is much simpler. But we would like to encourage pet lovers to question the aforementioned arguments critically, to think about them and decide what is best for the animals.

■ *"My Cottontail is the king of the guinea pigs!", Suzie says with pride.*

A rabbit which lives with a group of guinea pigs is still lonely. Without at least one animal of the same species, a rabbit or guinea pig will always be a single, lonely animal, even when living in a group of a different species.

Of course, a nice relationship between the two kinds of animals can develop, but only because they are lonely. Each animal has, instead of a companion of the same species, another life partner which was forced upon it and cannot understand its behaviourial pattern. At first, it can appear sweet when a rabbit licks the guinea pig and lies close to or on top of it. If you look closer, however, it becomes clear that they do this only because they have to live in close proximity and have no other choice, just like an individually-kept animal draws closer to a human. In my long experience in the Rabbit and Rodent Refuge, I have never seen a rabbit prefer the company of a guinea pig to that of another rabbit if it has the choice, even if it has been living alone with a guinea pig for years.

It is possible that there will be problems between your rabbit and guinea pig (eg trying to mate, biting, loud tapping or even killing). If these animals had the opportunity to live together in a large outdoor run, with companions of the same species, they would behave completely differently.

The habitat of rabbits and guinea pigs kept together

The habitat should be as large as possible, at least 10 square metres. This way it can be created practically, allowing rabbits and guinea pigs enough room to move around according to their instincts. The hutch needs to be appropriate for both animals too. It should have several floors and compartments so that the animals can avoid each other if they wish to do so. The entrance for the guinea pigs needs to be at ground level. Besides that it needs:

- Numerous hideouts, so that the guinea pigs are not run over by rabbits
- An open area where rabbits can dart
- Several elevated areas as resting places for rabbits
- A large shared and protected feeding area
- Many overhanging branches
- Several protective hideouts so that the guinea pigs can arrange their paths from hideout to hideout

As rabbits become territorial very quickly, guinea pigs should not be added at a later date. Keeping these animals together is only advisable if guinea pigs are placed first or at the same time as rabbits and can adjust from the beginning. Experience has shown that smaller rabbits are less compatible with guinea pigs than larger breeds.

At the Rabbit and Rodent Refuge we receive many comments from content pet owners, who confirm that their animals are livelier and show a distinctive social behaviour since they have added a companion for each of them.

13 Keeping rabbits and guinea pigs together

Keeping rabbits and guinea pigs together should be appropriate for both types of animal.

The rabbit and the area of controversy between meat production animals and pets

Keeping rabbits appropriately is a very complex problem. This book is directed at pet owners with the wish to make them aware of the correct way to keep pet rabbits. Without doubt there is much more work to do in other areas, such as in the breeding of rabbits for meat production and as laboratory animals. We will not touch on this aspect, as it is too complicated for this book.

We would, however, remind you that our retail behaviour can put pressure on the issue and could eventually have an effect on how animals are kept. We decide which kind of rabbit meat we buy, so with a little goodwill and imagination, even commercially-bred animals can be kept appropriately.

Photo: M. Hänni

If in doubt, ask!

We receive numerous calls at the Rabbit and Rodent Helpline every day. Here is a selection of the most frequently asked questions:

Adjustment

The partner of our Peter Rabbit has died. After integrating a new companion, they viciously attack each other at night in the hutch. Do I have to separate them?
You will not achieve anything by separating the animals at night. The adjustment will start every day anew. You should have an exit- and entry-safe run outside, so the animals do not have to be locked up into a small area at night.

Elisa and Benny are a couple in love. Can I now integrate another rabbit?
With two rabbits that are so intensely connected, a third animal would probably become an outsider. I suggest adding two new rabbits if you have enough room.

We have two dwarf rabbits and would now like to save the life of a commercially-bred animal. Can that work?
A rabbit with a calming influence in a group of dwarf rabbits can be useful for the balance of the group. If the gender is suitable for the group, there is nothing to stop you doing this.

We have two female rabbits. One of them is very dominant so we separate them at night. They keep attacking each other every day. What can I do?
Do not separate the animals! You are not doing them any favours. They become much more stressed if they have to establish the hierarchy every day again. You could also consider adding a castrated male.

I would like to give my Charly a female but am not sure if I have the nerves for it.
Before taking this step you ought to be sure that you are ready to accept the hierarchy fights at the beginning. It would be a shame if you give up after a few days. You would not do Charly or the new rabbit any favours.

We constantly hear that rabbits should have some time to sniff each other out through the bars of a cage. What do you think?
I am not in favour of this method. Much time is wasted and the fights for the hierarchy will still be quite harsh.

Help! My rabbit bites!
The most frequent reason for aggression is the lack of social contact with a companion or a habitat that is too small. Not enough challenges can be a further reason. Rabbits should always have fresh gnawing material in the form of branches and twigs.

Nutrition

One of our rabbits has died due to a tear in its stomach wall, even though the animals always had plenty of hay in the rack and despite feeding them greenery in the morning and grain at night. Why did this happen?
You can be lucky for years while feeding your animal wrongly. However, one day the rabbit rushes hungrily and greedily to the greenery and that's it. The day always has to start with fresh, dry hay and the 'dessert' in form of greenery a few hours later. This way, no rabbit can over-indulge on greenery.

I never give my animals too much greenery and only give it out twice a week, but still they get bloated. Do I have to stop completely?
You should give the greenery regularly on a daily basis, but only a few hours after the rabbits have received fresh hay.

My rabbits have a free run in the garden. Do I have to worry that they might eat yew or thuja?
No, you do not have to worry about that. A rabbit fed with varied food will not touch poisonous plants.

Can rabbits be given blue- or white-pine branches?
Yes, as a hideout or to create a new smell in the run. For gnawing, however, they prefer red pine.

What do I do if the water freezes in winter?
Put it in the hutch. It should not freeze there. Otherwise refill it three times a day.

Our run is so large that the grass keeps on growing. The rabbits are constantly eating. Do I have to worry about bloating?
Rabbits that have constant access to grass will not overeat, but they should be given a lot of fresh, good quality hay in the morning all the same.

One of our rabbits has problems with its teeth. Is it sufficient if I give it a fair amount of hard bread?
First of all, a visit to the vet is advised. Give the rabbits a large amount of tasty hay and fresh branches for gnawing every day to wear their teeth down. Bread should only be given to underweight animals as a supplement.

Care

Benjamin and Peter are always sitting in the rain, even though they have a hutch. Are they not in danger of catching a cold?
Instead of staying in the hutch, they prefer dry, open areas that are covered, like boxes put sideways and lined with plenty of hay, elevated protected areas or an open roof over the hutch.

Our rabbits dig like moles. Should we close the burrows so we can keep an eye on them?
No, that would be a shame. Digging is an important occupation for your animals and provides extra space. You can keep an eye on them at feeding time.

I have two lovely rabbit brothers. Is it really necessary to castrate them?
It is absolutely necessary, the quicker the better. Once they start fighting, the problem cannot be solved just with castration.

I have bought two female rabbits. Now one of them has become pregnant. Should I separate them?
No, it is best not to change anything. You should, however, let your vet check that the other rabbit is not really a male that should be castrated. Accept the temporarily increased temper of the pregnant female and start making arrangements regarding birth control for the young ones.

My vet has advised me to keep our rabbit on newspapers or cloths for a week after the castration, before integrating it back into the group. Will they then start attacking each other again?
You should follow the advice of the expert who performed the operation. Personally, I would reintegrate the castrated rabbit immediately into the group, so that they do not suffer the stress of readjustment. I would, however, check the operation area daily.

We are keeping rabbits together with guinea pigs. Do I have to feed them separately?
If the rabbits are dominant, then it is advisable. As far as the type of food is concerned, it is best to give them a quality guinea pig food with lots of vitamin C for both animals.

We have built an outdoor run of six square metres for our three rabbits. Now a friend wants to add her rabbit. Is the run big enough for four animals?
It will be very difficult for the newcomer to be integrated into a group of three established animals in this small habitat.

Can I get two older rabbits used to an outdoor run?
Of course. With intuition and careful daily observation it is possible. It would be advisable to undertake the change in warm weather.

Our outside run is large with a lot of grass. Should I put bark bedding down as well?
Areas protected from rain should be covered with dry bark bedding. This way you can clean the run easily, as urine and excrement do not get absorbed directly into the ground.

Our rabbits scare very easily and at the smallest noise they disappear into their hutch. What can I do?
Maybe there are not enough hideouts in the run, such as boxes positioned sideways or overhanging branches, where your rabbits feel protected.

I would like to know at what temperature it becomes dangerous for our rabbits outside?
If your animals can move around freely in a run of at least six square metres and it is well equipped with a lot of dry hay, hideouts and a hutch as a burrow, it will never be too cold. A large amount of energy food should be provided.

I have only female rabbits, but one always mounts the others. Could it be possible that it is a male?
This is possible, but females can also mount other rabbits. This can be due to hormones or an expression of dominance. I would integrate a castrated male, as this will be calming for the group.

We have a rabbit mother with daughter. Why are they so bitchy with each other? They have always been together.
If you have enough space, add a castrated male. This will relieve the situation.

We would like to build an outdoor run for our rabbits, but it is autumn and the nights can be fairly cool. Is this still possible?
If you offer your animals several dry places, a hutch, elevated areas and the like, provide a lot of hay and make sure the animals can move around freely, this is not a problem.

We have many foxes which come close to the run at night and scare our animals to death. What can we do?
You should provide plenty of protected areas like hideouts, a hutch and several niches where they can hide.

We are keeping rabbits with guinea pigs but feel that the guinea pigs are stressed. What do I have to do?
Provide as many elevated areas as possible where the rabbits love to be. Also let them have plenty of fresh gnawing material to keep them occupied. The guinea pigs require lots of hideouts.

We have a group of three rabbits, but Roger mainly stays with the guinea pigs and does not have much contact with the other rabbits. What shall we do?
It would be a good idea to integrate a suitable, not too dominant female for Roger.

We already have guinea pigs but would like to add rabbits. Will they adjust to each other?
Not all rabbits accept guinea pigs. It is best if they grow up with each other or are still young. Larger rabbits tend to accept guinea pigs reasonably well. It is, however, essential that the run is large and high enough and equipped according to the needs of both species.

We have a rabbit and a guinea pig in our flat. We would like to do the best for both but do not have enough room for another two animals. What do you suggest?
I would try to find a good place for your rabbit in an outdoor run with other rabbits and get another guinea pig as a companion for the one you already have.

I have been offered a mobile run of five square metres by our neighbour. Is this too small for two dwarf rabbits?
Mobile runs are neither break-in- nor escape-proof. You would have to lock the animals up in their hutch at night, which could lead to aggression. Besides that, mobile runs are never equipped very well. If you go down this route you will not enjoy your animals for very long.

We have followed your suggestions but our rabbits still always fight.
Check the following points:
- Is your run big enough; at least 6 square metres for three rabbits plus 2 square metres for each extra animal?
- Does your run have enough hideouts, such as crates - at least two hideouts for each animal?
- Are your animals occupied enough? Are there daily fresh branches to gnaw, material from the woods, earth mounds to dig in and items to stimulate them in the run?

Birth control

We have bought pair of rabbits which we do not want to separate. We have therefore decided on early castration. My vet tells me that this operation is not possible before the animals are four months old and I would have to separate the animals for now to avoid offspring. What should I do?
Not every good vet has this expert knowledge. You should find a person who is an expert in early castration for this special operation.

My Spotty has a false pregnancy almost every two weeks and becomes very restless. I would like to get her spayed but everybody advises me not to.
The decision to spay is correct. All you have to do now is to find a vet for whom this operation is not a problem.

I have had my male castrated. How long do I have to keep it separate from the other rabbits?
It depends on whether it was sexually mature when you had it castrated. If it was, then you need to keep it separate for at least ten days. After that, nothing normally happens anymore. If it was less than three months old and therefore not sexually mature, you can put it back in the group right away.

Our darling, a female rabbit, has lost its partner. It is five years old. Is it possible to mate the animal once more?
It is possible but not very sensible. It could cost your rabbit its life.

Can an old male rabbit be castrated?
Of course. With the anaesthesia methods available today, the risk of such an operation is minimal.

Where should one look for answers on how to keep rabbits?

For medical questions it is best to contact your vet. For questions regarding matters such as care, feeding and adjusting, you can always contact the Rabbit and Rodent Refuge.

The Rabbit and Rodent Helpline: 0900 57 52 31
(CHF 2.13/min)

This number is only available in Switzerland and only possible from a landline. All charges go towards the care-needing and homeless animals at the Rabbit and Rodent Refuge.

We will be happy to help with questions or problems concerning rabbit and guinea pig care. With our extensive experience in our veterinary practice, the Rabbit and Rodent Helpline, and Rabbit and Rodent Refuge, we can advise you expertly with regard to:

- What to consider before acquiring rabbits and guinea pigs
- Purchase or installation of an outdoor run or indoor vivarium
- Questions regarding feeding and care
- Behavioural problems
- Integration of an animal into a group or a new environment
- Illness of an animal. We can help you to assess if, and how quickly, you have to plan a visit to the vet, as we have broad knowledge and a great spectrum of medical experience available.

With the purchase of accessories and the use of the Rabbit and Rodent Helpline Service you help to support homeless animals. Many thanks.

A look behind the scenes of the Rabbit and Rodent Refuge

Unfortunately, people often get animals without thinking. After a short while they are abandoned or passed on. We would like to give you a little insight into our sometimes very sad work at the Rabbit and Rodent Refuge.

Monday 5th July 1999

- Mrs D from Baden brings in seven rabbits which are two weeks old. Her neighbour put the conventional cage with the rabbit mother in the sun, where she suffered heatstroke. Mrs St has no time to bring up the babies with a bottle. She signs a statement saying she will not keep rabbits in the future.

- A couple of years ago Mrs C from Rifferswil got two guinea pigs from our refuge. One died recently. Now she has to give up the surviving guinea pig, because she is not prepared to add a second one to it. According to our animal placing contract, she is not allowed to keep this animal on its own.

Tuesday 6th July 1999

- Mrs M from Lugano brings in seven rabbits, a mother with its six babies, plus one guinea pig. She is afraid that her outdoor run has too much sun and is too small in this heat. She has no alternative but to give the animals away.

Wednesday 7th July 1999

- Mrs Sch from Spreitenbach brings in five rabbits: one uncastrated male, a mother rabbit and its three offspring, which have been kept on a balcony in unsatisfactory conditions. The owner is moving and has also developed an allergy. The male animals are all castrated immediately upon arrival at the refuge to avoid further offspring.

Friday 9th July 1999

- Mr G from Zurich hands in a rabbit. It was a present for his wife, but she could not deal with it because it scratched and did not want to be cuddled.

Saturday 10th July 1999

- Mrs M from Nuolen brings in a rabbit which will not integrate into the group and is even at war with the guinea pigs. It must now be adjusted to a new companion, with expertise and much patience.
- Mrs B from Zurich handed over an uncastrated male rabbit because she said her husband had developed an allergy. Besides that, they are afraid of the cost of the castration.

Monday 12th July 1999

- Two uncastrated male guinea pigs are deposited anonymously in the pouring rain outside our Refuge.
- Mr T from Zurich brings in a male rabbit to be castrated whilst he goes on holiday, but then decides he does not really want it back.
- Mrs M from Zurich brings in two rabbits in a hamster cage. This has been their habitat for two years. They are unable to stand properly because their claws are so long. Mrs M bought the animals for her children but they are now grown up and moving out.

Tuesday 13th July 1999

- Mr F from Lenzburg hands over four uncastrated male guinea pigs that attack each other fiercely. He has lost his enjoyment of them and he does not think it is worth getting them castrated.
- Mrs T from Zug brings in a pregnant guinea pig. She bought it in a pet shop but does not want young ones. The pet shop will not take it back.

Wednesday 14th July 1999

- Mrs St from Bonstetten brings in her guinea pig. Its partner has died and she would rather not keep guinea pigs any more.

- Mrs J from Obfelden delivers her remaining rabbit, whose partner has died. It was a present and no one has the time to care for it.

- Mrs B from Dübendorf cannot find a place to leave her rabbit whilst going on holiday. As it does not really give her any pleasure anymore, she would rather give it to us.

The Rabbit and Rodent Refuge

We care for these and many other abandoned and homeless animals. We castrate the males and try to understand the characters of the various rabbits and guinea pigs so that we can find a suitable new home for them.

The most important part of our work is the re-homing of the animals in our care, as only the best homes are good enough for them.

- We would like to appeal to all pet lovers who are able to become active in animal protection to accept the enormous responsibility entrusted in us towards these creatures.

- We would like to appeal to people who have carefully considered the acquisition of animals, planned well ahead or already have the fundamental experience in dealing with them.

- We set great store in good advice and support, even after purchase.

- We only place animals that are healthy, neutered and treated for parasites, and which are already used to appropriate greenery feeding.

- Here you can get young and also older animals, as often a companion is required for an animal that has lost its partner.

- We suggest you keep at least three animals so that you can take your time to replace a deceased pet.

- If you want to add a really suitable rabbit to a group, it is advisable to let us know in writing the kind of rabbit you would like and the exact age, character and gender of your animals and maybe a photo of the run.

  This way we can contact you as soon as we find a suitable animal. (This is, of course, for interested people in Switzerland).

- We will not consider any interested party who wants to buy a cheap animal as quickly as possible or only wants it for their children.

Because species-appropriate runs are difficult to find or not available in pet shops, and not all animal lovers are good at DIY, the runs described in this book can be bought at the Rabbit and Rodent Refuge. With the purchase of accessories from our refuge you are also supporting homeless animals.

Unfortunately, we are not able to deliver abroad. As soon as we find a distributor for vivariums and runs, it will be published on our website.

We can be reached on the Rabbit and Rodent Helpline, but only within Switzerland: 0900 57 52 31
                (CHF 2.13/min. for the benefit of homeless animals)

Website

We would be delighted if you would visit our website, which contains useful information as well as offering the opportunity to order our books:

www.husbandry.ch

Appendix

Appreciation

We would like to thank Prof. Dr. A. Steiger, Prof. Dr. E. Isenbügel, Prof. Dr. J. Meyer, Dr. P. Cooper, Anita Oehy and Ursula Schick for their contributions, Trudy Hood and Sandra Collins for the translation, Deborah Curtis for editing, and Joan Kägi for proofreading. I would also like to thank Karin Bretscher, who relieves me at the Rabbit and Rodent Refuge as well as Nadja Brunner and Jessica Jetzer, who help in the practice.

Photos

Unless stated otherwise, all photos were taken by the author.

Sales and Advice 0900 57 52 31

(CHF 2.13/min. for the benefit of homeless animals), only for landline connections in Switzerland

Index

A
Abnormal behaviour   81
Acquirement   43, 91, **93ff**
Adjustment   **116ff**
Animal protection standards   78

B
Basic food   142
Basic needs   23ff
Bathing   162
Behaviour (see social behaviour)
– Change in behaviour   153ff
– Eating behaviour   120, 148ff
– Social behaviour **109ff**, 173
– Types of behaviour   23ff, **110ff**
Birth   133
Birth control   127ff
Bloating   140, 166
Boredom   30
Box   66ff
Branches   26, 67, 83, **149ff**
Bread   150
Breeding maturity   137
Building suggestions   56ff
Burrow   27ff, 63

C
Caecotrophs 141, 164
Cage   41, 78ff
Carrying   156
Castration   127ff
– Female animals   89, 132
– Male animals   127ff
Change   30, 70
Changes in feeding   147
Checks   154ff
– Daily   148, 154
– Monthly   155
– Teeth   158
– Weekly   155
Claws   161
Cleaning the run   71ff
Coccidia   163ff
Cold weather   37

Companions of the same species 109
Costs   34
Creating a run   61ff

D
Diarrhoea   157
Digestion   139ff
Digging   27, 87
Domestication   19ff
Dwarf rabbits   13ff

E
Early castration   130ff
Eating behaviour   120, 148ff
Eating caecotrophs 164
Elevated area   65
Enemies   15, 47
Enthusiasm   93ff
Establishing gender   135
Exercise   25ff, 38, 86
Extra feeding for ill animals   152

F
False pregnancy   89ff
Feeding area   53, 64ff
Feeding sequence   143, 145
Feeding: see Nutrition
Fertilisation   135
Fights for hierarchy   118
Free run   38
Fungal infection   162

G
Gentle adjustment   123ff
Gnawing   **26,** 84ff
Gnawing material   26, 67, 83, **149ff**
Grain (rabbit mix)   149
Group animals   **23ff**, 77, 109, 173
Groups   23ff, 109, 113ff, 169
– Adjustment   116ff, 123
– Combination   113ff
– Loners   115
– Putting together   113, 122

H
Habitat 33ff, 175
Handling 133ff
Hare 16ff
Hay 142ff
Health **153ff**
- Anal region 156ff
- Bathing 162
- Carrying 156
- Claws 161
- Cleanliness 153, 164
- Diarrhoea 157
- Fur care 160
- Infestation by mites 163
- Observation 153ff
- Parasites 156, **162ff**
- Teeth 26, 158ff
- Vaccinations 168
- Weight 160
Heat 36ff
Heatstroke 37, 167
Helpline 187
Hideout 28, 66, 72
Holidays 97
Hollow tree trunk 62, 67
House-trained 84
Hutch 53, **62ff,** 83, 87

I
Illness 168
Indoor keeping 77ff
- Animal welfare standards 78
- Cage 78
- Keeping in a room 82ff
Installation items **62ff,** 72
Installation mistakes 70

K
Keeping alone **24,** 31, 110, 115, 127, 169, 174
Keeping on a balcony 86
Keeping together **171ff**

L
Life expectancy 42

M
Maggots 156
Males, uncastrated 104
Mites 163
Mound 27, 69

N
Neighbours 46, 87
Newborn 133
Nutrition **139ff**
- Change in food 147
- Daily ration 147
- Digestion 140ff
- Erorrs 145, 157
- Feeding plan 145
- Gnawing material 26, 67, 83, **149**
- Grain 149
- Greenery 146ff
- Hay 142ff
- Herbivores 139
- Nurturing orphaned rabbits 152
- Rabbit mix 149
- Water 143ff
- Winter Feeding 151

O
Occupation 20ff, 26ff, 68, 149
Offspring 132
Outdoor keeping **33ff,** 90
- Outdoor run 35, **45ff,** 56
- Misunderstandings 41, 55, 70
- Planning 33
- Weather 36
Outdoor run requirements 35, **45ff**
- Cleaning 71
- Creation 61ff
- Feeding area 53, **64ff**
- Free run 38
- Handling 49
- Installation items **62ff,** 72
- Location 45
- Mistakes 41, 55, 70
- Planning and building 33, **45ff,** 56ff
- Safety 46ff, 57
- Size 46
- Sleeping den **53,** 62ff
- Types of run 50ff, 56
Overview 29

Index

P
Parasites   156, 162ff
Pet shops   102
Pipes   63, 67
Poisonous plants   147
Pregnancy   133

Q
Questions   179ff

R
Rabbit and Rodent Helpline   187
Rabbit and Rodent Refuge   189ff
Rabbit corner   82
Rain   37
Rearing orphans   152
Reproduction   127ff, 136
Responsibility   **98ff**
Rest   30
Rodent   26
Runs   50, 56
– Flat roof   51
– Open on top   52
– Pyramid   50

S
Safety   46ff, 57
– Break-in proof   47ff
– Break-out proof   46
Separation   124, 169
Sexual maturity   136
Shady areas   68
Snow   37, 49
Social contact   24, **109ff,** 122
Species-appropriate   19ff
Stomach overloading   140, **165**
Stress   163ff
Structure (see Installation)

T
Teeth   26, **158ff**
Tympany   140, **165ff**

U
Uterus cancer   90, 132

V
Vaccinations   168
Veterinarian   170

W
Water   143
Weaning age   13
Weather   36
Website   193
Weight   160
Wild rabbits   15
Winter   37
Winter feeding   151

Y
Young animals   134

About the author and her work

Ruth Morgenegg puts her heart and soul into the protection of animal rights. She has dedicated her life to the animals and their welfare. Her husband, a vet, is a huge and essential help, without whose active contribution it would be impossible to achieve the impact that her work has.

Ruth's special interest has always been towards the most helpless and placid pets – those who suffer most from the ignorance and lack of intuition of their owners: guinea pigs and rabbits. Her sympathy with those cute animals, which are very often used as toys, led to the foundation of the Rabbit and Rodent Refuge. This is where she rescues unwanted and abandoned guinea pigs and rabbits, cares for them and eventually re-homes them with a responsible new owner. Ruth has become an expert in questions of species-appropriate care through years of experience and intensive observation of these animals.

Ruth does not, however, just care for rabbits and guinea pigs. Many cats and kittens owe their new and beautiful homes to her mediating activities. She takes in cats of all ages from animal shelters that do not have many opportunities to re-house these animals (specifically shelters in the Italian part of Switzerland). Whether cats, rabbits or guinea pigs, many four-legged creatures in need of help find their way to Obfelden and can only be re-housed thanks to the infrastructure that has been set up there and the tireless efforts of the Morgeneggs.

Marianne Wengerek

Books by the same author

With vast expert knowledge and even more courage and commitment, Ruth Morgenegg tackles prejudice and provides precise information regarding the needs of guinea pigs, their biology and how to keep them appropriately for their species.

Extract of the introduction by Prof. Dr Ewald Isenbügel

ISBN 978-3-9522661-3-7

The address to contact: on our website **www.husbandry.ch** the section 'books' will take you to the address where you can order.